National Parks
and Conservation Association

Thomas C. Kiernan
President

Dear Reader:

Welcome to the National Parks and Conservation Association's national park guidebooks—a series designed to help you to discover America's most significant scenery, history, and culture found in the more than 370 areas that make up the U.S. National Park System.

The park system represents the best America has to offer for our natural, historical, and cultural heritage—a collection of resources that we have promised to preserve "unimpaired" for future generations. We hope that, in addition to giving you practical information to help you plan your visits to national park areas, these guides also will help you be a more aware, more responsible visitor to our parks. The cautions offered at the beginning of these guides are not to frighten you away but to remind you that we all have a role in protecting the parks. For it is only if each and every one of us takes responsibility that these special places will be preserved and available for future generations to enjoy.

For more than three-quarters of a century, the National Parks and Conservation Association has been America's leading citizen advocacy group working solely to protect the national parks. Whether fighting to preserve the wilderness character of Cumberland Island National Seashore, preventing the expansion of a major airport outside the Everglades, stopping a coal mine at Cumberland Gap, or defeating legislation that could lead to the closure of many national parks, NPCA has made the voices of its members and supporters heard in efforts to protect the resources of our national parks from harm.

We hope that you will join in our commitment. Remember: when you visit the parks, take only pictures, and leave only footprints.

1776 Massachusetts Avenue, N.W., Washington, D.C. 20036-1904
Telephone (202) 223-NPCA(6722) • Fax (202) 659-0650
♻ PRINTED ON RECYCLED PAPER

CONTENTS

NPCA National Park Guide Series

NATIONAL PARKS
AND CONSERVATION ASSOCIATION

GUIDE TO NATIONAL PARKS
PACIFIC REGION

Written and compiled by Russell D. Butcher for the National Parks and
Conservation Association and edited by Lynn P. Whitaker

NPCA is America's only private, nonprofit citizen organization dedicated solely
to protecting, preserving, and enhancing the U.S. National Park System. The
association's mission is to protect and enhance America's National Park System
for present and future generations.

Guilford, Connecticut

Photo credits: pages i, 9, 47, 53, 76 © Carr Clifton; pages iii, iv–v, 13, 33 © Willard Clay; pages 1, 4, 17, 30, 81, 93 © Laurence Parent; pages 18–19, 40, 50 © Jeff Foott; pages 21, 25, 45, 69, 83 © David Muench; page 27 © William Neill/Larry Ulrich Stock; pages 36, 39, 51, 57 © Larry Ulrich; page 41 © Scott T. Smith; pages 61, 85 © Fred Hirschmann.

Maps: © Trails Illustrated, a division of National Geographic Maps
Cover and text design: Adam Schwartzman
Cover photo: Waimoku Falls, Haleakala National Park, Hawaii (© David Muench)

Library of Congress Cataloging-in-Publication Data

Butcher, Russell D.
    National Parks and Conservation Association guide to national parks: Pacific region / written and compiled by Russell D. Butcher for the National Parks and Conservation Association ; and edited by Lynn P. Whitaker. —
1st ed.
        p. cm. —(NPCA national park guide series)
    ISBN 0-7627-0573-6
    1. National parks and preserves—California Guidebooks.
2. National parks and preserves—Hawaii Guidebooks. 3. National parks and preserves—American Samoa Guidebooks. 4. National parks and preserves—Guam Guidebooks. 5. California Guidebooks. 6. Hawaii Guidebooks. 7. American Samoa Guidebooks. 8. Guam Guidebooks.
    I. Whitaker, Lynn P. II. Title. III. Series.
F859.3.B88   1999
919.6—dc21   99-23822
                                                                              CIP

♻ Printed on recycled paper
Printed and bound in Quebec, Canada
First edition/First printing

1
9
13
21
27
33
41
47
53
61
69
81

Pacific Region

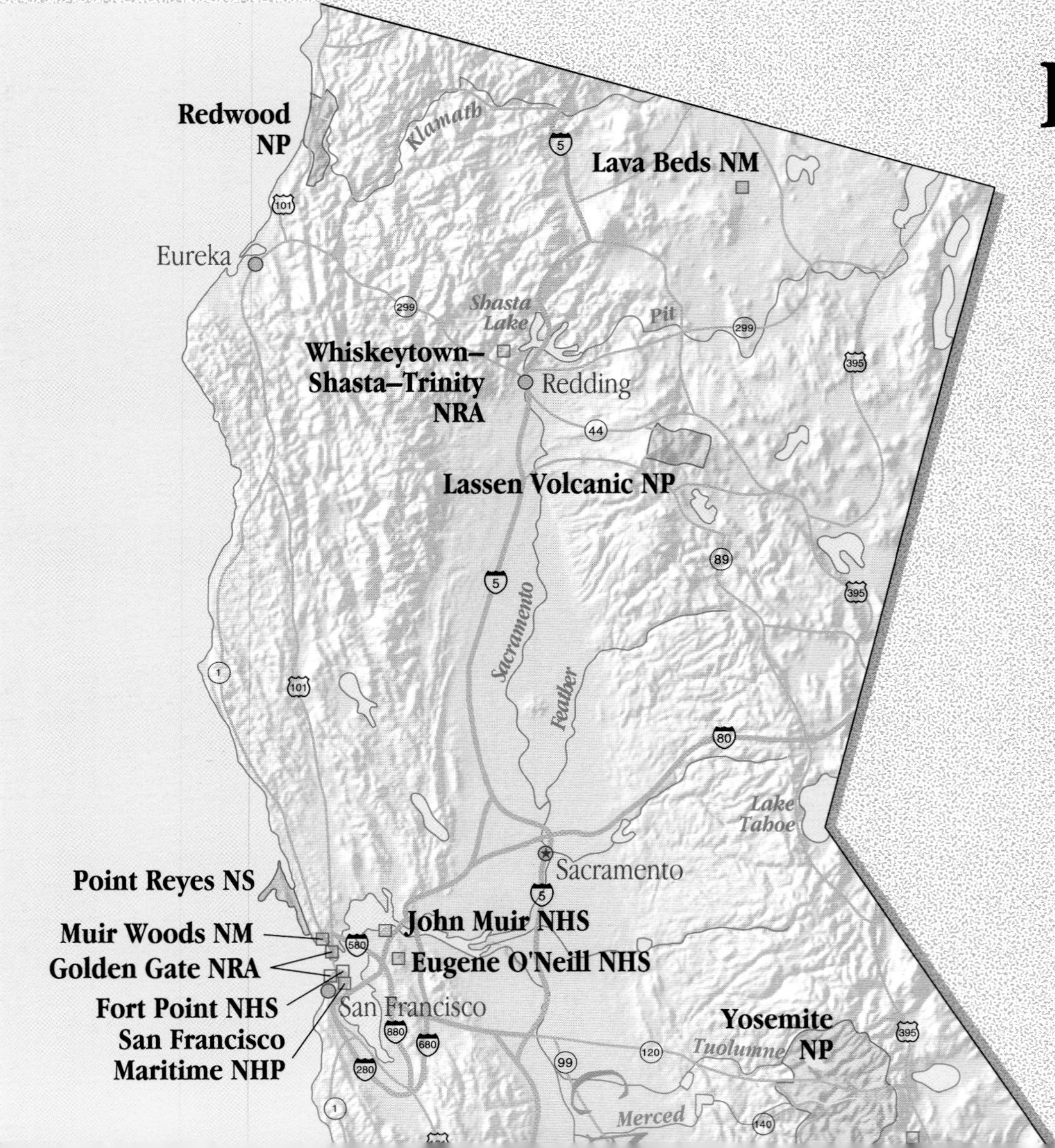

Redwood NP
Klamath
Lava Beds NM
Eureka
Shasta Lake
Pit
Whiskeytown–Shasta–Trinity NRA
Redding
Lassen Volcanic NP
Sacramento
Feather
Lake Tahoe
Sacramento
Point Reyes NS
Muir Woods NM
Golden Gate NRA
Fort Point NHS
San Francisco Maritime NHP
John Muir NHS
Eugene O'Neill NHS
San Francisco
Yosemite NP
Tuolumne
Merced
101
299
5
44
89
395
80
580
880
680
280
99
120
140
1

ABBREVIATIONS

NHP	National Historical Park
NHS	Natioanl Historic Site
N MEM	National Memorial
NM	National Monument
NMP	National Military Park
N PRES	National Preserve
NP	National Park
NRA	National Recreation Area
NS	National Seashore

0 50 100 Miles

0 50 100 150 Kilometers

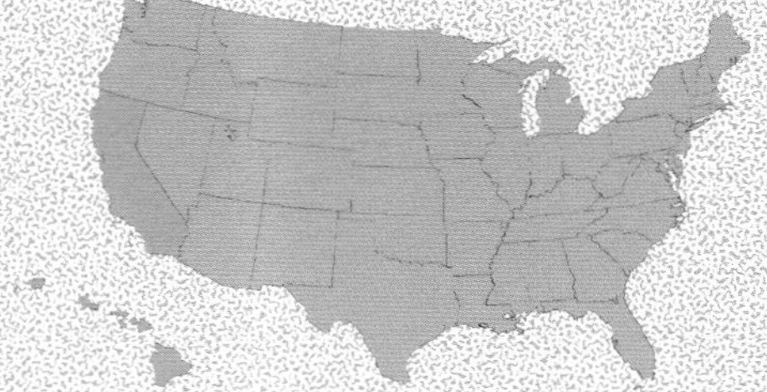

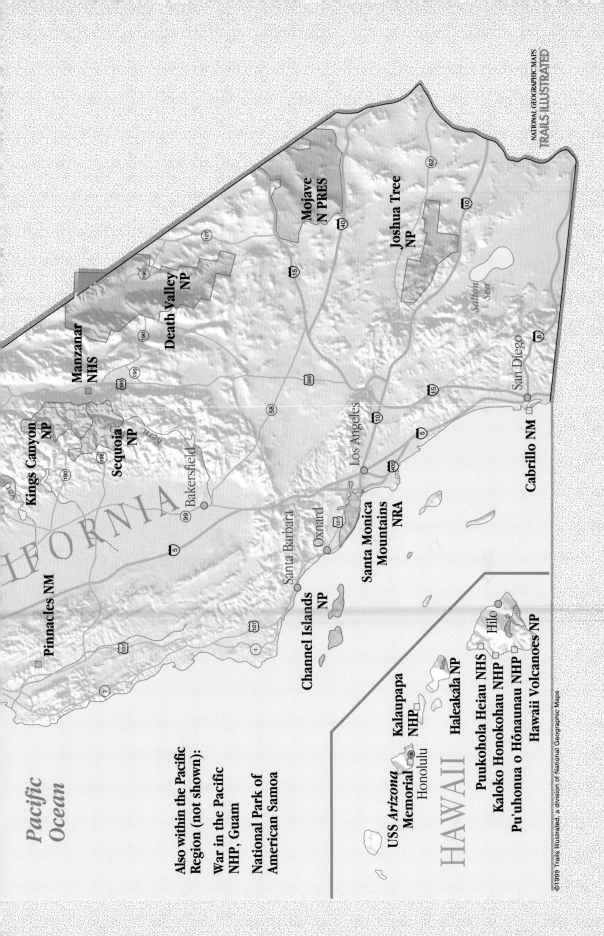

Pacific
Ocean

Also within the Pacific
Region (not shown):

War in the Pacific
NHP, Guam

National Park of
American Samoa

CALIFORNIA

Pinnacles NM

Kings Canyon
NP

Sequoia
NP

Bakersfield

Manzanar
NHS

Death Valley
NP

Mojave
N PRES

Joshua Tree
NP

Salton
Sea

Los Angeles

Santa Barbara

Oxnard

San Diego

Cabrillo NM

Channel Islands
NP

Santa Monica
Mountains
NRA

USS Arizona
Memorial

Honolulu

Kalaupapa
NHP

HAWAII

Haleakala NP

Puukohola Heiau NHS

Kaloko Honokohau NHP

Pu'uhonua o Hōnaunau NHP

Hawaii Volcanoes NP

Hilo

NATIONAL GEOGRAPHIC MAPS
TRAILS ILLUSTRATED

©1999 Trails Illustrated, a division of National Geographic Maps

▲ Coast, Kipahulu, Haleakala National Park, Maui, Hawaii

GENERAL INFORMATION

Whether you're an American history buff or a birdwatcher, a lover of rocky coastlines or marshy swamps, a dedicated environmentalist or a weekend rambler, and whether you're seeking a way to spend a carefully planned month-long vacation or an unexpectedly free sunny afternoon—the national parks are for you. They offer a broad spectrum of natural and cultural resources in all 50 states as well as Guam, Puerto Rico, the Virgin Islands, and American Samoa where you can learn, exercise, participate in activities, and be constantly moved and inspired by the riches available. Perhaps most important of all, as one of the National Park System's 280 million annual visitors, you become part of the attempt to preserve our natural and historical treasures for present and future generations.

This guidebook will help you do that, as one in a series of eight Regional National Park Guides covering all the units in the National Park System. This section of general information provides both an overview of key facts that can be applied to every unit and a brief history of the National Parks and Conservation Association.

SPECIAL PARK PASSES

Some parks charge entrance fees to help offset their operational costs. Several options for special entrance passes are available, enabling you to choose the most appropriate and economical way for you and your family and friends to visit sites.

Park Pass: For this annual entrance permit to a specific fee-charging park, monument, historic site, or recreation area in the National Park System, the cost is usually $10 or $15 depending on the area. Such a pass does not cover any fees other than entrance for permit holder and any accompanying passengers in a private noncommercial vehicle or, in the case of walk-in facilities, the permit holder's spouse, children, and parents. The pass may be pur-

chased in person or by mail from the unit at which it will be used. It is nontransferable and nonrefundable.

Golden Eagle Passport: This annual entrance pass admits visitors to all the federal lands that charge entrance fees; these include national parks, monuments, historic sites, recreation areas, national forests, and national wildlife refuges. The pass costs $50 and is valid for one year from purchase. It does not cover any fees other than entrance for permit holder and any accompanying passengers in a private noncommercial vehicle or, in the case of walk-in facilities, the holder's spouse, children, and parents. The Golden Eagle Passport may be purchased in person or by mail from the National Park Service, Office of Public Inquiries, Room 1013, U.S. Department of the Interior, 18th & C Streets, N.W., Washington, DC 20240 (202-208-4747) or at any of the seven National Park Service field offices, any of the nine U.S. Forest Service regional offices, or any national park unit and other federal areas that charge an entrance fee. It is nontransferable and nonrefundable.

Golden Age Passport: A one-time $10 fee for this pass allows lifetime entrance to all federal fee-charging areas as described in the Golden Eagle Passport section for citizens and permanent residents of the United States who are 62 years of age or older and any accompanying passengers in a private noncommercial vehicle or, in the case of walk-in facilities, the holder's spouse and children. This pass also entitles the holder to a 50 percent discount on use fees charged in park areas. The Golden Age Passport must be obtained IN PERSON at any of the locations listed in the Golden Eagle Passport section; mail requests are not accepted. Applicants must provide proof of age, such as a driver's license or birth certificate, or sign an affidavit attesting to eligibility.

Golden Access Passport: This free lifetime entrance permit to all federal fee-charging areas as described in the Golden Eagle Passport section is available for citizens and permanent residents of the United States who are visually impaired or permanently disabled and any accompanying passengers in a private noncommercial vehicle or, in the case of walk-in facilities, the permit holder's spouse, children, and parents. It also entitles the holder to a 50 percent discount on use fees charged in park areas. The Golden Access Passport must be obtained IN PERSON at any of the locations listed in the Golden Eagle Passport section; mail requests are not accepted. Applicant must provide proof of eligibility to receive federal benefits or sign an affidavit attesting to one's eligibility.

PASSPORT TO YOUR NATIONAL PARKS

The *Passport to Your National Parks* is a special commemorative item designed to serve as a companion for park visitors. This informative and unique publication records each visit through special regional and national stamps and cancellations. When you visit any national park, be sure to have your Passport canceled with a rubber stamp marking the name of the park and the date you were there. The Passport gives you the opportunity to share and relive your journey through America's national parks and will become a travel record to cherish for years. Passports cost $4.95; a full set of ten national and regional stamps are $3.95. The national parks represented in the stamp set vary from year to year. For ordering information, call 800-821-2903, or write to Eastern National Park & Monument Association, 110 Hector Street, Suite 105, Conshohocken, PA 19428.

HELPFUL TRIP-PLANNING PUBLICATIONS

Two volumes offer descriptive text on the National Park System: *Exploring Our National Parks and Monuments,* by Devereux Butcher (ninth edition by Russell D. Butcher), and *Exploring Our National Historic Parks and Sites,* by Russell D. Butcher. These books feature descriptions and black-and-white photographs of more than 370 National Park System units. Both volumes also contain chapters on possible new parks, threats to the parks, a history of NPCA, and the national

park standards. To order, contact Roberts Rinehart Publishers, 6309 Monarch Park Place, Niwot, CO 80503; 800-352-1985 or 303-530-4400.

NPCA offers the following brochures at no charge: *The National Parks: How to Have a Quality Experience* and *Visiting Battlefields: The Civil War.* These brochures provide helpful information on how best to enjoy a visit to the national parks. NPCA members can also receive the *Park System Map and Guide, The National Parks Index, The National Parks Camping Guide,* and *Lesser Known Areas* as part of NPCA's PARK-PAK by calling 202-223-6722, ext. 214.

The Story Behind the Scenery® and *The Continuing Story*® series are lavishly illustrated books providing informative text and magnificent photographs of the landscapes, flora, and fauna of our national parklands. More than 100 titles on the national parks, historic events, and Indian cultures, as well as an annual national parks calendar, are available. For information, call toll free 800-626-9673, fax to 702-731-9421, or write to KC Publications, 3245 E. Patrick Lane, Suite A, Las Vegas, NV 89120.

The National Parks: Index and *Lesser Known Areas,* both produced by the National Park Service, can be ordered by contacting the Superintendent of Documents, U.S. Government Printing Office, Washington, DC 20402-9325; 202-512-1800. To receive at no charge the *National Park System Map and Guide,* the *National Trails System Map and Guide;* or an *Official Map and Guide* of specific national parks, contact National Park Service, Office of Information, P.O. Box 37127, Washington, DC 20013-7127; 202-208-4747.

National Parks Visitor Facilities and Services is a directory of vendors authorized to serve park visitors through contracts with the National Park Service. Concessionaires offering lodging, food, beverages, outfitting, tours, trail rides, and other activities and services are listed alphabetically. To order, contact the National Park Hospitality Association, 1331 Pennsylvania Ave., N.W., Suite 724, Washington, DC 20004; 202-662-7097.

▲ *Misty Bridalveil Creek, Yosemite National Park, California*

Great Walks, Inc., publishes six pocket-sized books of detailed information on specific trails in Yosemite; Sequoia and Kings Canyon in California; Big Bend; Great Smoky Mountains; and Acadia and Mount Desert Island in Maine. For information, send $1 (refundable with your first order) to Great Walks, P.O. Box 410, Goffstown, NH 03045.

The U.S. Bureau of Land Management (BLM) offers free maps that detail recreation areas and scenic and backcountry roads and trails. These are available by contacting the BLM at the Department of the Interior, 1849 C St., N.W., Suite 5600, Washington, DC 20240; 202-452-5125. In addition, *Beyond the National Parks: A Recreational Guide to Public Lands in the West,* published by the Smithsonian Institution Press, is an informative guidebook to many special places administered by the BLM. *America's Secret Recreation Areas,* by Michael Hodgson, is an excellent resource for little-known natural areas in 12 Western states. It details 270 million acres of land administered by BLM, with campgrounds, recreational activities, trails, maps, facilities, and much more. The 1995-96 edition is published by Foghorn Press and is available for $17.95 by calling 1-800-FOGHORN.

The National Wildlife Refuge Visitors Guide can be ordered free from the U.S. Fish and Wildlife Service's Publications Unit at 4401 North Fairfax Dr., MS 130 Webb, Arlington, VA 22203; 703-358-1711.

The four-volume *Birds of the National Parks* by Roland H. Wauer, a retired NPS interpreter and biologist, provides an excellent reference on the parks' birds and their seasons and habitats. This series, written for the average rather than specialist park visitor, is unfortunately out of print.

SAFETY AND REGULATIONS

To protect the national parks' natural and cultural resources and the millions of people who come to enjoy them, the National Park Service asks every visitor to abide by some important regulations. Park staffs do all they can to help you have a safe and pleasant visit, but your cooperation is essential.

Some park hazards—deep lakes, sheer cliffs, extremely hot or cold temperatures—cannot be eliminated. However, accidents and illnesses can be prevented if you use the same common sense you would at home and become familiar with the park. Take some time before your trip or when you first arrive to get to know the park's regulations, warnings, and potential hazards. If you have children, make sure they understand such precautions, and keep a careful watch over them, especially in potentially dangerous situations. If you are injured or become ill, the staff can help by directing you to the nearest medical center and, in some parks, by giving you emergency care.

A few rules and safety tips are common to many parks. At all parks, you must keep your campsite clean and the park free of litter by disposing of refuse in trash receptacles. The National Park Service also asks you to follow federal regulations and refrain from the abuse of alcohol and the use of drugs, which are often contributing factors to injuries and deaths. Other rules and safety tips are outlined in the "Special Advisories and Visitor Ethics" section; more detailed information may be provided in park brochures, on signs, and on bulletin boards at camping areas and other park sites. The National Park Service asks that you report any violation of park regulations to park authorities. If you have any questions, seek the advice of a ranger.

SPECIAL ADVISORIES AND VISITOR ETHICS

Safe Driving

Park roads are designed for sightseeing, not speeding. Because roads are often narrow and winding and sometimes steep, visitors should drive carefully, observe posted speed limits, and be alert for wildlife, pedestrians, bicyclists, other drivers, fallen rocks or trees, slippery roads, and other hazards. Be especially alert for motorists who might stop unexpectedly for sightseeing or wildlife viewing. Visitors are urged to use roadside pullouts instead of stopping on the roadway.

Campfires

Most parks permit fires, as long as certain rules are followed. To avoid a wildfire that would be dangerous to people, property, and natural resources, parks may allow only certain types of campfires—fires only in grills provided, for example, or in designated fire rings. Firewood gathering may be prohibited or restricted to certain areas, so visitors should plan on bringing their own fuel supply. Fires should be kept under control, should never be left unattended, and should be thoroughly extinguished before departure.

Quiet Hours

Out of respect for other visitors, campers should keep noise to a minimum at all times, especially from 10 p.m. to 6 a.m.

Pets

Pets must always be leashed or otherwise physically restrained for the protection of the animal, other visitors, and wildlife. Pets may be prohibited from certain areas, including public buildings, trails, and the backcountry. A few parks prohibit pets altogether. Dog owners are responsible for keeping their pets quiet in camping areas and elsewhere. Guide dogs are exempted from park restrictions. Some parks provide kennel services; contact the park visitor center for information.

Protection of Valuables

Theft is just as much a problem in the national parks as elsewhere, so when leaving a campsite or heading out on a trail, visitors should take valuables along or hide them out-of-sight in a locked vehicle, preferably in the trunk.

Heat, Cold, and Other Hazards

Visitors should take precautions to deal with the demands and hazards of a park environment. On hot days, pace yourself, schedule strenuous activities for the morning and evening hours, and drink plenty of water and other fluids. On cold days or if you get cold and wet, frostbite

and the life-threatening illness called hypothermia can occur, so avoid subjecting yourself to these conditions for long periods. In the thinner air of mountains and high plateaus, even those tasks easy to perform at home can leave one short of breath and dizzy; the best advice is to slow down. If a thunderstorm occurs, avoid exposed areas and open bodies of water, where lightning often strikes, and keep out of low-lying areas and stream beds, where flash floods are most likely to occur.

Wild Plants and Animals

It is the responsibility of every visitor to help preserve the native plants and animals protected in the parks: leave them as you find them, undisturbed and safe. Hunting or carrying a loaded weapon is prohibited in all national parks and national monuments. Hunting during the designated season is allowed in parts of only a few National Park System areas, such as national recreation areas, national preserves, and national seashores and lakeshores. While biting insects or toxic plants, such as poison ivy or poison oak, are the most likely danger you will encounter, visitors should be aware of hazards posed by other wild plants and animals. Rattlesnakes, ticks, and animals carrying rabies or other transmittable diseases, for instance, inhabit some parks. Any wild creature—whether it is as large as a bison or moose or as small as a raccoon or prairie dog—is unpredictable and should be viewed from a distance. Remember that feeding any wild animal is absolutely prohibited.

Campers should especially guard against attracting bears to their campsites as a close encounter with a grizzly, brown, or black bear can result in serious injury or death. Park officials in bear country recommend, and often require, that campers take certain precautions. One is to keep a campsite clean. Bears' sensitive noses can easily detect food left on cans, bottles, and utensils or even personal items with food-like odors (toothpaste, deodorant, etc.). Second, food items should be stored in containers provided by the parks or in your vehicle, preferably out of sight in the trunk. Bears, especially those in Yosemite, are adept at breaking into cars and other motor vehicles containing even small amounts of food and can cause extensive damage to motor vehicles as they attempt to reach what they can smell. Third, in the backcountry, food should be hung from poles or wires that are provided or from a tree; visitors should inquire at the park as to the recommended placement. In treeless surroundings, campers should store food at least 50 yards from any campsite. If bears inhabit a park on your itinerary, ask the National Park Service for a bear brochure with helpful tips on avoiding trouble in bear country and inquire if bears are a problem where you plan to hike or camp.

Backcountry Camping

Camping in the remote backcountry of a park requires much more preparation than other camping. Most parks require that you pick up a backcountry permit before your trip so that rangers will know about your plans. They can also advise you of hazards and regulations and give you up-to-date information on road, trail, river, lake, or sea conditions, weather forecasts, special fire regulations, availability of water, and other matters. Backcountry permits are available at visitor centers, headquarters, and ranger stations.

There are some basic rules to follow whenever you camp in the backcountry: stay on the trails; pack out all trash; obey fire regulations; be prepared for sudden and drastic weather changes; carry a topographic map or nautical chart when necessary; and carry plenty of food and water. In parks where water is either unavailable or scarce, you may need to carry as much as one gallon of water per person per day. In other parks, springs, streams, or lakes may be abundant, but always purify water before drinking it. Untreated water can carry contaminants. One of the most common, especially in Western parks, is *giardia*, an organism that causes an unpleasant intestinal illness. Water may have to be boiled or purified with tablets; check with the park staff for the most effective treatment.

Sanitation

Visitors should bury human waste six to eight inches below ground and a minimum of 100 feet from a watercourse. Waste water should be disposed of at least 100 feet from a watercourse or campsite. Do not wash yourself, your clothing, or your dishes in any watercourse.

CAMPING RESERVATIONS

Most campsites are available on a first-come, first-served basis, but many sites can be reserved through the National Park Reservation Service. For reservations at Acadia, Assateague Island, Cape Hatteras, Channel Islands, Chickasaw, Death Valley, Everglades, Glacier, Grand Canyon, Great Smoky Mountains, Greenbelt, Gulf Islands, Joshua Tree, Katmai, Mount Rainier, Rocky Mountain, Sequoia-Kings Canyon, Sleeping Bear Dunes, Shenandoah, Whiskeytown, and Zion, call 800-365-CAMP. For reservations for Yosemite National Park, call 800-436-PARK. Reservations can also be made at any of these parks in person. Currently, reservations can be made as much as eight weeks in advance or up to the day before the start of a camping stay. Please have credit card and detailed camping information available when you call in order to facilitate the reservation process.

BIOSPHERE RESERVES AND WORLD HERITAGE SITES

A number of the national park units have received international recognition by the United Nations Educational, Scientific and Cultural Organization for their superlative natural and/or cultural values. Biosphere Reserves are representative examples of diverse natural landscapes, with both a fully protected natural core or park unit and surrounding land being managed to meet human needs. World Heritage Sites include natural and cultural sites with "universal" values that illustrate significant geological processes, may be crucial to the survival of threatened plants and animals, or demonstrate outstanding human achievement.

CHECKLIST FOR HIKING AND CAMPING

Clothing

Rain gear (jacket and pants)
Windbreaker
Parka
Thermal underwear
T-shirt
Long pants and shorts
Extra wool shirt and/or sweater
Hat with brim
Hiking boots
Camp shoes/sneakers
Wool mittens
Lightweight shoes

Equipment

First-aid kit
Pocket knife
Sunglasses
Sunscreen
Topographic map
Compass
Flashlight, fresh batteries, spare bulb
Extra food & water (even for short hikes)
Waterproof matches
Fire starter
Candles
Toilet paper
Digging tool for toilet needs
Day backpack
Sleeping bag
Sleeping pad or air mattress
Tarp/ground sheet
Sturdy tent, preferably free-standing
Insect repellent
Lip balm
Pump-type water filter/water purification tablets
Water containers
Plastic trash bags
Biodegradable soap
Small towel
Toothbrush
Lightweight backpack stove/extra fuel
Cooking pot(s)
Eating utensils
Can opener
Electrolyte replacement for plain water (e.g., Gatorade)
Camera, film, lenses, filters
Binoculars
Sewing kit
Lantern
Nylon cord (50 feet)
Whistle
Signal mirror

A Brief History

▲ *Giraud Peak, Kings Canyon National Park, California*

A Brief History of the National Parks and Conservation Association

In 1916, when Congress established the National Park Service to administer the then nearly 40 national parks and monuments, the agency's first director, Stephen Tyng Mather, quickly saw the need for a private organization, independent of the federal government, to be the citizens' advocate for the parks.

Consequently, on May 19, 1919, the National Parks Association—later renamed the National Parks and Conservation Association (NPCA)—was founded in Washington, D.C. The National Park Service's former public relations director, Robert Sterling Yard, was named to lead the new organization—a position he held for a quarter century.

The association's chief objectives were then and continue to be the following: to vigorously oppose threats to the integrity of the parks; to advocate worthy and consistent standards of *national* significance for the addition of new units to the National Park System; and, through a variety of educational means, to promote the public understanding and appreciation of the parks. From the beginning, threats to the parks have been a major focus of the organization. One of the biggest conservation battles of NPCA's earliest years erupted in 1920, when Montana irrigation interests advocated building a dam and raising the level of Yellowstone Lake in Yellowstone National Park. Fortunately, this threat to the world's first national park was ultimately defeated—the first landmark victory of the fledgling citizens' advocacy group on behalf of the national parks.

At about the same time, a controversy developed over the authority given to the Water Power Commission (later renamed the Federal Power Commission) to authorize the construction of hydropower projects in national parks. The commission had already approved the flooding of Hetch Hetchy Valley in Yosemite National Park. In the ensuing political struggle, NPCA pushed for an amendment to the water power law that would prohibit such projects in all national parks. A compromise produced only a partial victory: the ban applied to the parks then in existence, but not to parks yet to be established. As a result, each new park's enabling legislation would have to expressly stipulate that the park was exempt from the commission's authority to develop hydropower projects. Yet this success, even if partial, was significant.

Also in the 1920s, NPCA successfully urged establishment of new national parks: Shenandoah, Great Smoky Mountains, Carlsbad Caverns, Bryce Canyon, and a park that later became Kings Canyon, as well as an expanded Sequoia. The association also pushed to expand Yellowstone, Grand Canyon, and Rocky Mountain national parks, pointing out that "the boundaries of the older parks were often established arbitrarily, following ruler lines drawn in far-away offices." The association continues to advocate such topographically and ecologically oriented boundary improvements for many parks.

In 1930, the establishment of Colonial National Historical Park and the George Washington Birthplace National Monument signaled a broadening of the National Park System to places of primarily historical rather than environmental importance. A number of other historical areas, such as Civil War battlefields, were soon transferred from U.S. military jurisdiction to the National Park Service, and NPCA accurately predicted that this new category of parks "will rapidly surpass, in the number of units, its world-celebrated scenic" parks. Today, there are roughly 200 historical parks out of the total of 378 units. NPCA also pushed to add other units, including Everglades National Park, which was finally established in 1947.

A new category of National Park System units was initiated with the establishment of Cape Hatteras National Seashore in North Carolina. However, in spite of NPCA opposition, Congress permitted public hunting in the seashore—a precedent that subsequently opened the way to allow this consumptive resource use in other national seashores, national lakeshores, national rivers, and national preserves. With the exception of traditional, subsistence hunting in Alaska national preserves, NPCA continues to oppose hunting in all national parks and monuments.

In contrast to its loss at Cape Hatteras, NPCA achieved a victory regarding Kings Canyon National Park as a result of patience and tenacity. When the park was established in 1940, two valleys—Tehipite and Cedar Grove—were left out of the park as a concession to hydroelectric power and irrigation interests. A few years later, however, as the result of concerted efforts by the association and other environmental groups, these magnificently scenic valleys were added to the park.

In 1942, the association took a major step in its public education mission when it began publishing *National Parks.* This award-winning, full-color magazine contains news, editorials, and feature articles that help to inform members about the parks, threats facing them, and opportunities for worthy new parks and offers readers a chance to participate in the protection and enhancement of the National Park System.

In one of the most heavily publicized park-protection battles of the 1950s, NPCA and other groups succeeded in blocking construction of two hydroelectric power dams that would have inundated the spectacularly scenic river canyons in Dinosaur National Monument. In the 1960s, an even bigger battle erupted over U.S. Bureau of Reclamation plans to build two dams in the Grand Canyon. But with the cooperative efforts of a number of leading environmental organizations and tremendous help from the news media, these schemes were defeated, and Grand Canyon National Park was expanded.

In 1980, the National Park System nearly tripled in size with the passage of the Alaska National Interest Lands Conservation Act (ANILCA). One of the great milestones in the history of American land conservation, ANILCA established ten new, and expanded three existing, national park units in Alaska. This carefully crafted compromise also recognized the special circumstances of Alaska and authorized subsistence hunting, fishing, and gathering by rural residents as well as special access provisions on most units. The challenge of ANILCA is to achieve a balance of interests that are often in conflict. Currently, NPCA is working to protect sensitive park areas and wildlife from inappropriate development of roads and unregulated motorized use, and to ensure that our magnificent national parks in Alaska always offer the sense of wildness, discovery, and adventure that Congress intended.

In 1981, the association sponsored a conference to address serious issues affecting the welfare of the National Park System. The following year, NPCA published a book on this theme called *National Parks in Crisis.* In the 1980s and 1990s, as well, the association sponsored its nationwide "March for Parks" program in conjunction with Earth Day in April. Money raised from the hundreds of marches funds local park projects, including improvement and protection priorities and educational projects in national, state, and local parks.

NPCA's landmark nine-volume document, *National Park System Plan,* was issued in 1988. It contained proposals for new parks and park expansions, assessments of threats to park resources and of research needs, explorations of the importance of interpretation to the visitor's quality of experience, and issues relating to the internal organization of the National Park Service. Two years later, the two-volume *Visitor Impact Management* was released. This document found favor within the National Park Service because of its pragmatic discussions of "carrying capacity" and visitor-impact management methodology and its case studies. In 1993, *Park Waters in Peril* was released, focusing on threats seriously jeopardizing water resources and presenting a dozen case studies.

The association has become increasingly concerned about the effect of noise on the natural quiet in the parks. NPCA has helped formulate restrictions on flightseeing tours over key parts of the Grand Canyon; urged special restrictions on tour flights over Alaska's national parks; supported a ban on tour flights over other national parks such as Yosemite; expressed opposition to plans for construction of major new commercial airports close to Mojave National Preserve and Petroglyph National Monument; opposed the recreational use of snowmobiles in some parks and advocated restrictions on their use in others; and supported regulations prohibiting the use of personal watercraft on lakes in national parks.

Other association activities of the late 20th

century have included helping to block development of a major gold mining operation that could have seriously impaired Yellowstone National Park; opposing a coal mine near Zion National Park that would have polluted Zion Canyon's North Fork of the Virgin River; objecting to proposed lead mining that could pollute the Ozark National Scenic Riverways; opposing a major waste dump adjacent to Joshua Tree National Park; and helping to defeat a proposed U.S. Department of Energy nuclear waste dump adjacent to Canyonlands National Park and on lands worthy of addition to the park. NPCA is currently proposing the completion of this national park with the addition of 500,000 acres. This proposal to double the size of the park would extend protection across the entire Canyonlands Basin. NPCA has also continued to work with the Everglades Coalition and others to help formulate meaningful ways of restoring the seriously impaired Everglades ecosystem; is urging protection of New Mexico's geologically and scenically outstanding Valles Caldera, adjacent to Bandelier National Monument; and is pushing for the installation of scrubbers on air-polluting coal-fired power plants in the Midwest and upwind from the Grand Canyon.

The association, in addition, is continuing to seek meaningful solutions to traffic congestion and urbanization on the South Rim of the Grand Canyon and in Yosemite Valley; is opposing construction of a six-lane highway through Petroglyph National Monument that would destroy sacred Native American cultural assets; and is fighting a plan to build a new road through Denali National Park. NPCA has supported re-establishment of such native wildlife as the gray wolf at Yellowstone and desert bighorn sheep at Capitol Reef and other desert parks, as well as urging increased scientific research that will enable the National Park Service to more effectively protect natural ecological processes in the future. The association is also continuing to explore a proposal to combine Organ Pipe Cactus National Monument and Cabreza Prieta National Wildlife Refuge into a Sonoran Desert National Park, possibly in conjunction with Mexico's Pinacate Biosphere Reserve.

In 1994, on the occasion of NPCA's 75th anniversary, the association sponsored a major conference on the theme "Citizens Protecting America's Parks: Joining Forces for the Future." As a result, NPCA became more active in recruiting a more racially and socially diverse group of park protectors. Rallying new constituencies for the parks helped NPCA in 1995 to defeat a bill that would have called for Congress to review national parks for possible closure. NPCA was also instrumental in the passage of legislation to establish the National Underground Railroad Network to Freedom.

In January 1999, NPCA hosted another major conference, this time focusing on the need for the park system, and the Park Service itself, to be relevant, accessible, and open to all Americans. The conference led to the creation of a number of partnership teams between national parks and minority communities. In conjunction with all this program activity, the association experienced its greatest growth in membership, jumping from about 24,000 in 1980 to nearly 400,000 in the late 1990s.

As NPCA and its committed Board of Trustees, staff, and volunteers face the challenges of park protection in the 21st century, the words of the association's past president, Wallace W. Atwood, in 1929 are as timely now as then:

> *All who join our association have the satisfaction that comes only from unselfish acts; they will help carry forward a consistent and progressive program . . . for the preservation and most appropriate utilization of the unique wonderlands of our country. Join and make this work more effective.*

Each of us can help nurture one of the noblest endeavors in the entire history of mankind—the national parks idea that began so many years ago at Yellowstone and has spread and blossomed around the world. Everyone can help make a difference in determining just how well we succeed in protecting the priceless and irreplaceable natural and cultural heritage of the National Park System and passing it along unimpaired for the generations to come.

DEATH VALLEY NATIONAL PARK

▲ *Moon over Manly Beacon and Panamint Ridge*

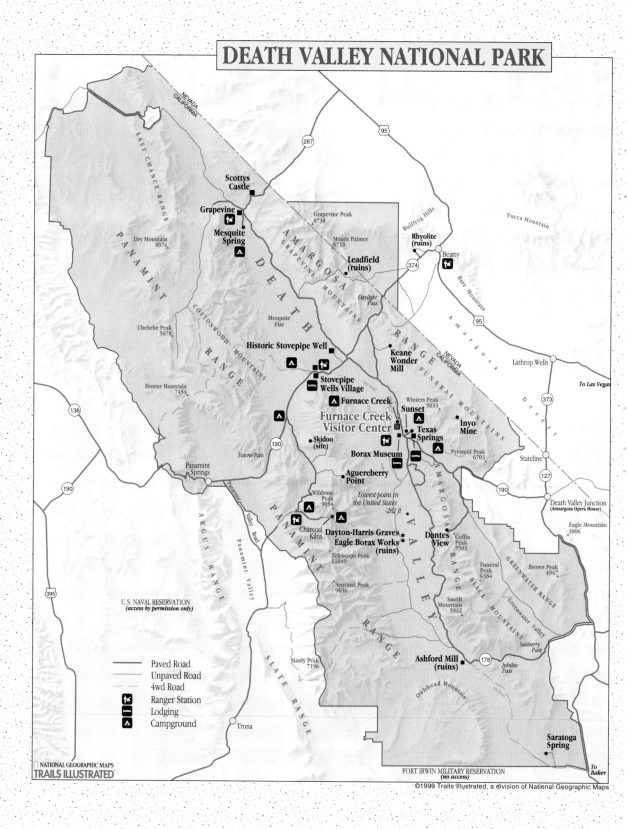

DEATH VALLEY NATIONAL PARK

NEVADA
CALIFORNIA

Last Chance Range

Dry Mountain
8674

PANAMINT

Scottys
Castle

Grapevine

Mesquite
Spring

Cottonwood Mountains

Ubehebe Peak
5678

Hunter Mountain
7454

Historic Stovepipe Well

Stovepipe
Wells Village

Furnace Creek

Furnace Creek
Visitor Center

Skidoo
(site)

Towne Pass

Panamint
Springs

Aguereberry
Point

Wildrose
Peak
9054

Charcoal
Kilns

Dayton-Harris Graves
Eagle Borax Works
(ruins)

Telescope Peak
11049

Sentinel Peak
9636

Manly Peak
7196

SLATE RANGE

Trona

Grapevine Peak
8738

Mount Palmer
6710

AMARGOSA

GRAPEVINE MOUNTAINS

Leadfield
(ruins)

Daylight
Pass

Mesquite
Flat

DEATH

VALLEY

Keane
Wonder
Mill

Winters Peak
5033

Sunset

Texas
Springs

Borax Museum

Lowest point in
the United States
-282 ft

RANGE

FUNERAL MOUNTAINS

NEVADA
CALIFORNIA

Inyo
Mine

Pyramid Peak
6703

Dantes
View

Coffin
Peak
5503

Smith
Mountain
5912

AMARGOSA RANGE

BLACK MOUNTAINS

Funeral
Peak
6384

Ashford Mill
(ruins)

Owlshead Mountain

95

267

374

95

Bullfrog Hills

Rhyolite
(ruins)

Beatty

Bare Mountain

Amargosa

Yucca Mountain

Lathrop Wells

To Las Vegas

Desert

373

Stateline

127

190

Death Valley Junction
(Armargosa Opera House)

Eagle Mountain
3806

Brown Peak
4947

GREENWATER RANGE

Greenwater Valley

Salsberry
Pass

178

Jubilee
Pass

Saratoga
Spring

To
Baker

U.S. NAVAL RESERVATION
(access by permission only)

ARGUS RANGE

Panamint Valley

PANAMINT

Panamint Valley Road

136

190

395

Paved Road
Unpaved Road
4wd Road
Ranger Station
Lodging
Campground

FORT IRWIN MILITARY RESERVATION
(no access)

NATIONAL GEOGRAPHIC MAPS
TRAILS ILLUSTRATED

©1999 Trails Illustrated, a division of National Geographic Maps

DEATH VALLEY NATIONAL PARK

P.O. Box 579
Death Valley, CA 92328-0579
760-786-2331

Death Valley's name is foreboding. Yet, in this awesome, 120-mile-long, mountain-framed desert basin, visitors can enjoy spectacular spring wildflowers, beautifully wind-sculpted sand dunes, expanses of salt flats, colorful rock formations and canyons, the remains of historic mining activities, extensive sloping *bajadas* of gravel and rocks washed down from the mountains, and rugged mountain ranges occasionally snow-capped in winter.

This great national park encompasses 3,367,627 acres, mostly in eastern California, with a small part extending into Nevada. Elevations range from 282 feet below sea level up to 11,049 feet above sea level on the highest summit of the Panamint Mountains. Death Valley is the hottest desert area in the world, with summer maximum temperatures consistently higher than anywhere else on earth. The highest temperature recorded in the valley was 134 degrees Fahrenheit in the shade. But, despite the harshness and severity of the environment, many species of wildlife and more than 900 kinds of plants have adapted to the intense heat and dryness.

A presidential proclamation established Death Valley as a national monument in 1933. In 1984, it was designated part of the Mojave and Colorado Deserts Biosphere Reserve. After many years in which NPCA and other environmental groups advocated enhanced protection because of this unique area's natural and historical values, the monument was finally expanded in 1994 and designated a national park under the California Desert Protection Act.

huge pluvial lake that existed in Death Valley from 25,000 to 50,000 years ago, part of the bed of which is now a vast salt flat covered with several-foot-high salt-encrusted spires and pinnacles; **Mesquite Flat Sand Dunes**, graceful rolling "waves" of sand that contrast with the jagged features of distant mountains; the dune- and saltmarsh-edged ponds at **Saratoga Springs**, a peaceful oasis at the southern end of the valley; **Zabriskie Point**, a scenic view of erosion-sculpted, colorful clay hills and ridges in Furnace Creek Wash; **Golden Canyon**, a narrow, winding gorge of yellow rock formations and a section of red cliffs called the **Red Cathedral**; the 2,400-foot-diameter and 750-foot-deep **Ubehebe Crater**, created 1,000 years ago during a violent volcanic eruption; **Harmony Borax Works**, the remains of the first successful borax-processing operation in Death Valley, dating from 1883; **Ashford Mill**, the ruins of a place where gold ore was once processed; **Wildrose Canyon**, which features abandoned, stone charcoal kilns constructed more than 100 years ago; **Scotty's Castle**, an ornate, Moorish-style mansion built in 1922 for $2.5 million as a vacation retreat for wealthy midwesterner Albert Johnson, who named it for Walter Scott, a frequent visitor; **Dante's View** atop the Black Mountains, which provides an awesome panorama 6,000 feet into the vastness of Death Valley and westward across to the Panamint Range; **Aguereberry Point**, a viewing spot more than 6,500 feet above the valley floor which offers a spectacular panorama eastward toward the Black and Funeral mountains; and the park's highest point, reachable by trail from Mahogany Flat Campground in the Panamint Mountains, the 11,049-foot **Telescope Peak**, where a stand of ancient bristlecone pines grows on the summit.

OUTSTANDING FEATURES

Among the many outstanding features of the park are the following: **Badwater**, a small, spring-fed, saline pond near the lowest point in the Western hemisphere, at 282 feet below sea level; **Devil's Golf Course**, the remains of a

ACTIVITIES

Auto tours, hiking, birdwatching, photography, bicycling, horseback riding, interpretive exhibits, guided tours, picnicking, and camping. Further information is available in the park's newspaper, *Death Valley National Park—A Guide for the Visitor.*

When to Go

The park is open year-round. From October until May, the climate is generally mild and pleasant, with average daily temperatures between 40 and 90 degrees. From November to March, the weather is ideal: moderate temperatures combined with cloudless days and clear air. Occasional winter storms bring life-giving rain, while windstorms are common in the spring. In the summer, it is extremely and oppressively hot, with daytime temperatures commonly over 120 degrees Fahrenheit.

How to Get There

By Car: There are a number of possible routes. The park's west entrance is reached from U.S. Route 395 at Red Mountain, traveling north 23 miles on an unnumbered highway, then north 56 miles on CA Route 178 and east into the park. From U.S. Route 395 at Lone Pine, it is 19 miles southeast on CA Route 136 and east about 20 miles on CA Route 190. The park's southeast entrance is reached from I-15 at Baker, traveling north 58 miles on CA Route 127 and west about ten miles on CA Route 178 to the park. Three other east entrances are reached from U.S. Route 95 in Nevada: Furnace Creek entrance from Amargosa Valley, Nevada, traveling south 16 miles on NV Route 373 and seven miles on CA Route 127 to Death Valley Junction, then west 18 miles on CA Route 190. This entrance can also be reached from I-15 at Baker, traveling north 74 miles on CA Route 127 to Death Valley Junction, and west 18 miles on CA Route 190. From Beatty, Nevada, it is about nine miles to the park. From Scotty's Junction, it is about 20 miles to the Grapevine Canyon entrance. Note: There are still many miles of driving from park entrances to the visitor center and facilities, such as overnight lodgings and restaurants.

By Air: McCarran International Airport in Las Vegas and Los Angeles International Airport (LAX) are served by numerous national and regional airlines.

By Train: Amtrak (800-872-7245) stops in Las Vegas and Barstow, California.

By Bus: Greyhound Lines (800-231-2222) stops in Barstow.

Fees and Permits

Entrance fees are $10 per vehicle and are valid for seven consecutive days. Fees are charged for tours of Scotty's Castle; tickets are sold on a first-come, first-served basis.

Visitor Centers and Museums

Furnace Creek Visitor Center: Open daily year-round. Interpretive exhibits, audiovisual programs, publications, maps, activities schedule, interpreter-guided walks, naturalist talks, and evening programs. There is a historical museum at Furnace Creek Ranch.

Facilities

Lodging, dining room, restaurants, snack services, gift shops, post office, picnic areas, campgrounds, and hot showers.

Handicapped Accessibility

Accessible services and facilities are located in the Furnace Creek area. Sunset campground has 16 accessible sites near wheelchair-accessible restrooms. Furnace Creek and Mesquite Springs campgrounds have wheelchair-accessible restrooms. The TTY phone number is 619-786-2471.

Medical Services

Emergency first aid is available from ranger medics. Air and ground ambulance service is available. The nearest hospitals are in Las Vegas and Tonopah, Nevada, and in Lone Pine, California.

Pets

Pets must be leashed at all times; leashes are not to exceed six feet in length. Pets are not allowed in the visitor center, other public buildings, or the backcountry.

Safety and Regulations

The harsh desert environment of heat, aridity, and vast distances of Death Valley makes it necessary to take special precautions when visiting this park:

▲ *Scotty's Castle, Death Valley National Park, California*

- In summer, avoid traveling during the hottest time of the day, and read the Death Valley Guide for safe travel suggestions.

- When driving, check vehicle gauges frequently; especially keep a sharp eye on the fuel gauge and carry extra water.

- At any time of year, CARRY A GENEROUS SUPPLY OF WATER.

- It is not advised to hike into backcountry alone; always tell someone where you are going and when you expect to return.

- Be alert for abandoned-mine hazards, exercise special care when driving or walking in the vicinity of all mine workings, and never enter abandoned mines.

For the protection of the park, several additional precautions are necessary:

- Roadside camping and firewood gathering are prohibited.

- Fires are permitted only in campstoves or grills.

- All vehicles must stay on designated roads, and firearms must be cased or otherwise rendered inoperative.

- Remember that it is illegal to feed, hunt, capture, or in any other way harm or disturb wildlife or to collect, cut, or damage trees, plants, or other natural or historic objects.

▲ Sand dunes, Death Valley National Park, California

Lodging and Dining

Options include:

Furnace Creek Inn, a historic Spanish mission-style hotel dating from 1927, offering comfortable rooms, from October to May. Natural thermal-spring-fed pool, elegant dining room, bar, entertainment, dancing, concierge, gift shop, lighted tennis courts, golf, exercise equipment, sauna, lawn games, and library. For information and reservations, call 619-786-2361.

Furnace Creek Ranch, offering a variety of rooms year-round. Restaurants, groceries, laundry, gift shop, golf course, pool, lawn games, historical museum, and guided tours. For information and reservations, call 800-528-6367.

Stovepipe Wells Village Motel, offering rooms year-round. Pool, restaurant, and gift shop. For information and reservations, call 619-786-2387.

A restaurant and gift shop are also located at Scotty's Castle.

Campgrounds

Summer temperatures soar above 120 degrees, but during the rest of the year campers enjoy generally mild, sunny weather. Some camping areas are desert oases with shade trees and water, others are on the open desert, and a couple are in the mountains. All sites are available on a first-come, first-served basis, except Furnace Creek and Texas Springs group sites, which are available for reservations early November through late April via National Park Reservation Service at 800-365-CAMP. For the rest of the year, reservations for group camping may be made by contacting the park.

The following times are particularly popular and congested: Martin Luther King, Jr., Day; President's Day; Easter week; Death Valley 49ers Encampment (the second weekend in November); Thanksgiving weekend; and the week between Christmas Day and New Year's Day. You may wish to plan your visit at less-crowded times of year.

Backcountry Camping

Backcountry camping is on a first-come, first-served basis. It is recommended from October through May.

FLORA AND FAUNA (Partial Listings)

Mammals: Desert bighorn sheep, mule deer, mountain lion, bobcat, coyote, gray and kit foxes, spotted skunk, ringtail, blacktail jackrabbit, desert and Nuttall's cottontail, round-tailed and California ground squirrels, white-tailed antelope squirrel, Panamint chipmunk, and kangaroo and pack rats. Feral burros also inhabit the park.

Birds: Of the nearly 300 species of birds that live in or migrate through Death Valley, there are mallard, pied-billed grebe, killdeer, Gambel's and mountain quail, red-tailed hawk, golden eagle, kestrel, prairie falcon, great horned and burrowing owls, turkey vulture, roadrunner, mourning dove, black-chinned and broad-tailed hummingbirds, flicker, Say's phoebe, white-throated swift, violet-green swallow, raven, scrub and pinyon jays, mountain chickadee, plain titmouse, rock wren, mockingbird, LeConte's thrasher, robin, Townsend's solitaire, mountain bluebird, loggerhead shrike, phainopepla, warblers (yellow-rumped, yellowthroat, and orange-crowned), Brewer's and red-winged blackbirds, great-tailed grackle, lesser goldfinch, sparrows (black-throated, chipping, rufous-crowned, Brewer's, song, and savannah), rufous-sided and green-tailed towhees, and house finch.

Amphibians and Reptiles: Desert tortoise, desert toad, Pacific treefrog, desert banded gecko, lizards (collared, desert side-blotched, Panamint alligator, gridiron-tailed, Mohave sand, and horned), chuckwalla, and 18 kinds of snakes, including red racer, rosy boa, lyre, coachwhip, western patch-nosed, gopher, common kingsnake, long-nosed, western shovel-nosed, western black-headed, and the sidewinder and Panamint rattlesnakes.

Trees, Shrubs, and Flowers: Some of the more than 900 species of plants recorded in the park are pines (bristlecone, limber, and singleleaf pinyon), Utah and western junipers, Fremont cottonwood, honey and screwbean mesquites, Rocky Mountain maple, smoke tree, Joshua tree and Mojave yucca, mountain mahogany, creosotebush, brittlebush, desert holly, turtleback, iodine bush, eucnide, desert velvet, four-winged saltbush, ephedra, greasewood, wetleaf, desert "fir", arrowweed, Death Valley sage (salvia), pickleweed, desert trumpet, Inyo prince's-plume, Chinese lantern, rock-nettle, mojavea, phacelias (Fremont, notch-leaf, and caltha-leaf), desertgold, desert fivespot, poppies (prickly, pygmy, and desert gold), rocklady, Shockley goldenhead, desert sunflower, coreopsis, senecio, desert star, primroses, paintbrush, globemallow, limestone penstemon, tackstem, 20 kinds of gilias, Panamint daisy, and 13 species of cacti, including beavertail, strawtop cholla, mound, cottontop, fishhook, and calico.

NEARBY POINTS OF INTEREST

The areas surrounding Death Valley National Park offer many exciting natural and historical attractions that can be enjoyed as day trips or overnight excursions. To the south are the Mojave National Preserve and Joshua Tree National Park. To the east, in Nevada, are Ash Meadows National Wildlife Refuge, adjacent to which is the Devils Hole unit of Death Valley National Park; Lake Mead National Recreation Area; Valley of Fire State Park; the Mt. Charleston unit of the Toiyabe National Forest; and the U.S. Bureau of Land Management's Red Rock Canyon National Conservation Area. To the west are the Inyo, Sequoia, and Sierra national forests, Sequoia-Kings Canyon National Parks, the Alabama Hills, and Manzanar National Historic Site.

HALEAKALA NATIONAL PARK

▲ Waimoku Falls

HALEAKALA NATIONAL PARK

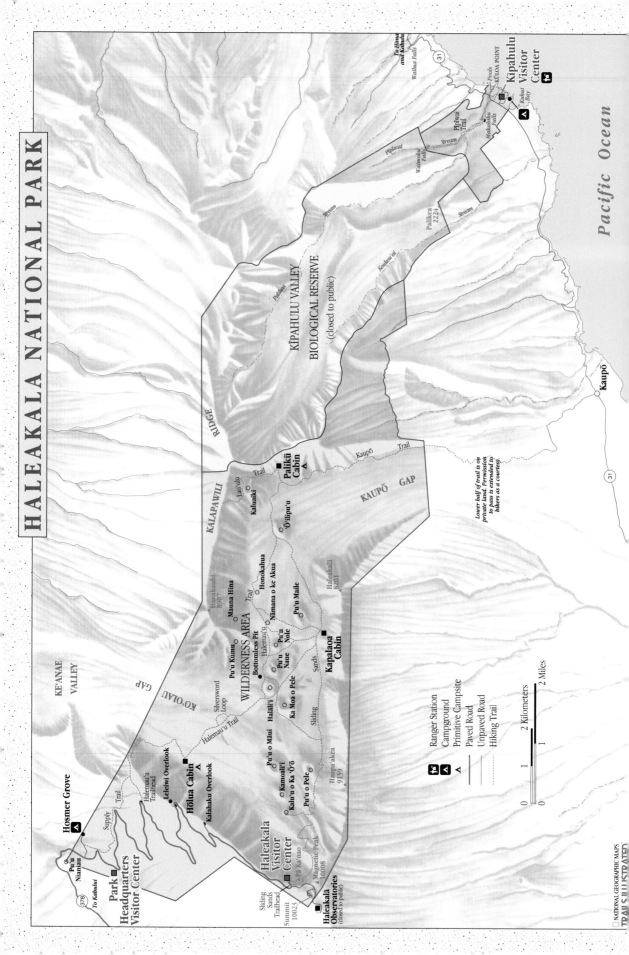

Pacific Ocean

Kipahulu Visitor Center

KĪLOA POINT
Kukui Bay

Pipiwai Trail

Makahiku Falls

Waimoku Falls
Stream

Pipiwai

Stream

Palikea 2224

Stream

Koukowai

KIPAHULU VALLEY

BIOLOGICAL RESERVE
(closed to public)

Palikea

RIDGE

Kaupō

KALAPAWILI

Kaupō Trail

Palikū Cabin

KAUPŌ GAP

Trail
Lauʻulu
Kaluaiki
Haleakalli 8201

Lower half of trail is on private land. Permission to pass is extended to hikers as a courtesy.

Oʻilipuʻu

Hamakanhi 8907
Mauna Hina
Honokahua
Nāmana o ke Akua
Puʻu Maile

Trail
Halemauʻu
Puʻu Kumu
Bottomless Pit
Puʻu Nole
Puʻu Naue

WILDERNESS AREA

Kapalaoa Cabin

Sands

KEʻANAE VALLEY

KOʻOLAU GAP

Silversword Loop
Halaliʻi
Ka Moa o Pele
Sliding

Halemauʻu Trail
Puʻu o Maui
Kamoaliʻi
Kaluʻu o Ka ʻŌʻō
Puʻu o Pele
Haupaʻakea 9159

Hosmer Grove

Supply Trail

Halemauʻu Trailhead
Leleiwi Overlook
Hōlua Cabin
Kalahaku Overlook

Puʻu Nianiau

Park Headquarters Visitor Center

Haleakalā Visitor Center

Sliding Sands Trailhead

La Pa Ka ʻoao
Magnetic Peak 10008
Summit 10023
Haleakala Observatories (closed to public)

(378)
To Kahului

(31)

To Hana and Kahului
Waituu Falls

(31)

Legend

Ranger Station
Campground
Primitive Campsite
Paved Road
Unpaved Road
Hiking Trail

0   1   2 Kilometers
0   1   2 Miles

NATIONAL GEOGRAPHIC MAPS
TRAILS ILLUSTRATED

HALEAKALA NATIONAL PARK

P.O. Box 369
Makawao, HI 96768-0369
808-572-9306

This park was established on the Hawaiian island of Maui to protect the outstanding features of 10,000-foot-high Haleakala ("House of the Sun") Volcano, including the huge, moonscape-like, cinder cone-studded, 2,720-foot-deep basin at its summit. The most recent volcanic eruptions occurred on the southwestern flank of the mountain around 1790, while the most recent eruptions within the basin itself were apparently a few centuries ago. The 28,091-acre park also protects the unique and fragile ecosystems and rare biotic species of the lush, rainforest-filled Kipahulu Valley (which receives extra protection within a closed-to-entry biological reserve), along with the magical pools and waterfalls along 'Ohe'o Gorge and a short stretch of Pacific Ocean coast. The park was established as part of Hawaii National Park in 1916, and then in 1961, it was made a separate national park. Much of the park was designated in 1976 as wilderness; and in 1980, the park was named a Biosphere Reserve.

Even with these protections, a new challenge has arisen over the past decade. Since the mid-1980s, there has been a rapidly growing number of helicopter airtour overflights creating a substantial and unacceptable level of noise for people and animals on the ground. As a consequence, NPCA is strongly urging the implementation of meaningful controls on these flights over both Haleakala and Hawaii Volcanoes national parks.

OUTSTANDING FEATURES

Among the many outstanding features of the park are the following: **Haleakala Crater**, an awesome, colorful basin of cinder cones and lava flows, reached by **Halemauu** and a number of other looping trails; **Silversword**, a spectacular plant that resembles the yuccas and agaves of the American Southwest with its many dagger-like leaves covered with silvery, silky hairs; **Pele's Paint Pot**, an area of spectacular colors caused by the variety of minerals in the lava; **Hosmer Grove**, a cool, shady grove of such non-native trees as Douglas fir, redwood, and eucalyptus and a popular place for picnicking and camping between the main entrance and park headquarters; The Nature Conservancy's **Waikamoi Preserve**, an ecologically rich area reached on guided walks from Hosmer Grove which provides habitat for such birds as native Hawaiian honeycreepers (one species of which is the striking, bright-crimson i'iwi with black-wings and sharply curved beak); **Pu'u Ulaula** ("red hill") which, at 10,023 feet elevation, is the highest point in the park and a place where park staff present interpretive talks; and **Waimoku Falls**, a 300-foot-high, rainforest-surrounded waterfall in the lower part of Kipahulu Valley, reached by **Pipiwai Trail** that begins just below the State Route 31 bridge across 'Ohe'o Stream and climbs for about two miles, passing 184-foot **Mahahiku Falls** and a series of delightful pools and smaller waterfalls.

ACTIVITIES

Hiking, guided walks and talks, birdwatching, swimming, horseback riding, auto tours, interpretive exhibits, picnicking, and camping. Further information is available in the park's newspaper, *Ka Leo O Halealaka—The Voice of Haleakala*.

PRACTICAL INFORMATION

When to Go

The park is open year-round. Weather near the summit varies considerably: summers are generally dry and moderately warm, but come prepared for occasional cold, windy, damp weather. Winters tend to be cold, wet, foggy, and windy. Generally, a mixture of all kinds of weather occurs in the spring and fall.

How to Get There

By Car: From State Route 36 to Haleakala Crater, take State Route 37 (Haleakala Highway) to just beyond Pukalani, State Route 377, and then steeply climbing Haleakala Crater Rd. into the park and up to the crater rim. To reach the coastal area of the park, take the Hana Highway (State Routes 36 and 360), through Hana and Koali.

By Air: Kahului Airport (808-872-3800) is served by many commercial airlines. IslandAir serves Hana Airport (808-248-8208).

Fees and Permits

Fees to the summit area are $10 per vehicle and are valid for 7 consecutive days; there are no fees in the coastal area of the park. Free permits, available at park headquarters, are required for backcountry camping in the summit area.

Visitor Center

Haleakala Visitor Center: Open daily year-round, sunrise to 3 p.m. Closed Christmas Day. Interpretive exhibits, wilderness protection and other interpretive programs, bookstore with publications, maps, and schedules.

Facilities

Restrooms, picnic areas, marked trails, drinking water.

Handicapped Accessibility

Park headquarters, visitor center, summit building, ranger stations, and Hosmer Grove are wheelchair accessible. There are accessible toilets at Kipahulu campground.

Medical Services

First aid is available in the park. Maui Memorial Hospital is closest to the summit, the Kaiser Clinic is 30 miles away in Kahului, and the Hana Medical Clinic is ten miles away in Hana.

Pets

Pets are permitted on leashes, not to exceed six feet in length, but are prohibited in the backcountry, on trails, and in public buildings.

Safety and Regulations

For your safety and enjoyment and for the protection of the park, please follow these regulations and suggestions:

- Roads are often narrow, steep, and winding, so drive slowly and carefully.

- Because the weather is unpredictable and can be either cold and wet or hot and sunny, bring appropriate clothing and gear.

- Never hike alone, and always let someone know where you're going and when you expect to return.

- Stay well back from waterfalls, and stay on marked trails to avoid causing erosion and damage to plantlife.

- Regulations prohibit the removal of volcanic rocks, plants, and other natural objects.

- Building wood fires is also not permitted.

- Special cautions for swimmers: Never swim in streams during high water. If the water level is rising fast, promptly get out as streams can become raging torrents in minutes. Take care when walking on muddy banks and wet rocks. Check carefully before diving or jumping into pools, for in some places, submerged ledges are near the pool's edge.

OVERNIGHT STAYS

Lodging and Dining

No overnight accommodations or food services are available within the park. Lodging and meals are available in Kula, Pukalani, Hana, Ka'anapali, Lahaina, and elsewhere.

Campgrounds

Campers stay either amid the volcanic, desert-like landscape of lava ash flows and cinder cones of Haleakala Wilderness Area or in the contrasting lush green coastal areas of grasslands and rainforests.

Campgrounds are open all year on a first-come, first-served basis. Each camping party is limited to a maximum of 12 people, and camping is limited to three nights per month,

▲ Silversword, Haleakala National Park, Hawaii

camping and cabins combined, with no more than two nights at any site. In addition, a person may camp three nights per month in both Hosmer Grove and Kipahulu campgrounds. Each of three primitive cabins at Paliku, Kapalaoa, and Holua has a wood-burning stove, cooking utensils and dishes, 12 padded bunks, pit toilets, and limited water and firewood. Reservations are required and must be received by mail at least two months prior to the first day of the month for which you are requesting a reservation. Reservations are issued by a monthly lottery.

Backcountry Camping

Holua and Paliku are open all year on a first-come, first-served basis. A free backcountry permit is required. Each site accommodates up to 25 people, and camping parties are limited to 12 people. The total permitted length of stay in the backcountry is three nights per month. Occasionally, drinking water is not available at backcountry sites; check with the park for up-to-date information.

FLORA AND FAUNA (Partial Listings)

Mammals: Asian mongoose, Hawaiian hoary bat, Hawaiian monk seal, spinner dolphin, and humpback whale.

Birds: Hawaiian (dark-rumped) petrel, nene (Hawaiian goose), 'io (Hawaiian hawk), black and gray francolins, chukar, ring-necked pheasant, Pacific golden plover, wandering tattler, spotted and zebra doves, pueo (short-eared owl), barn owl, Eurasian skylark, 'elepaio (Hawaiian flycatcher), Japanese bush-warbler, 'oma'o (Hawaiian thrush), melodious laughing-thrush, red-billed leiothrix, common myna, Japanese white-eye, northern cardinal, house finch, amakihi, Maui creeper, and several honeycreepers: 'i'iwi, akohekohe, and 'apapane.

Trees, Shrubs, and Flowers: 'ohi'a (an upland tree with scarlet, pompon-like blossoms), koa (an acacia tree), pandanus, mamane (palila tree), wiliwili, guava, sandalwood, bamboo, koali, kupaoa, pilo, pukiawe and 'ohelo berry (two alpine shrubs), taro, tarweed, geranium, morning glory, odorless mint, silversword, a'a'u and other ferns, and bunchgrass.

NEARBY POINTS OF INTEREST

The areas surrounding Haleakala National Park offer a number of interesting natural and historical attractions that can be enjoyed as day trips or overnight excursions. Waianapanapa State Park is about 35 miles away, in Hana; and 'Iao Valley State Park, with 2,250-foot-high 'Iao Needle, is about 40 miles away, in Wailuku. On the Big Island of Hawaii are Puukohola Heiau National Historic Site, Kaloko-Honokohau National Historical Park, Pu'uhonua o Honaunau National Historical Park, and Hawaii Volcanoes National Park. On Molokai is Kalaupapa National Historical Park, and on Oahu is the USS Arizona Memorial.

Hawaii Volcanoes National Park

▲ Lava flow from Pu'u O'o Vent

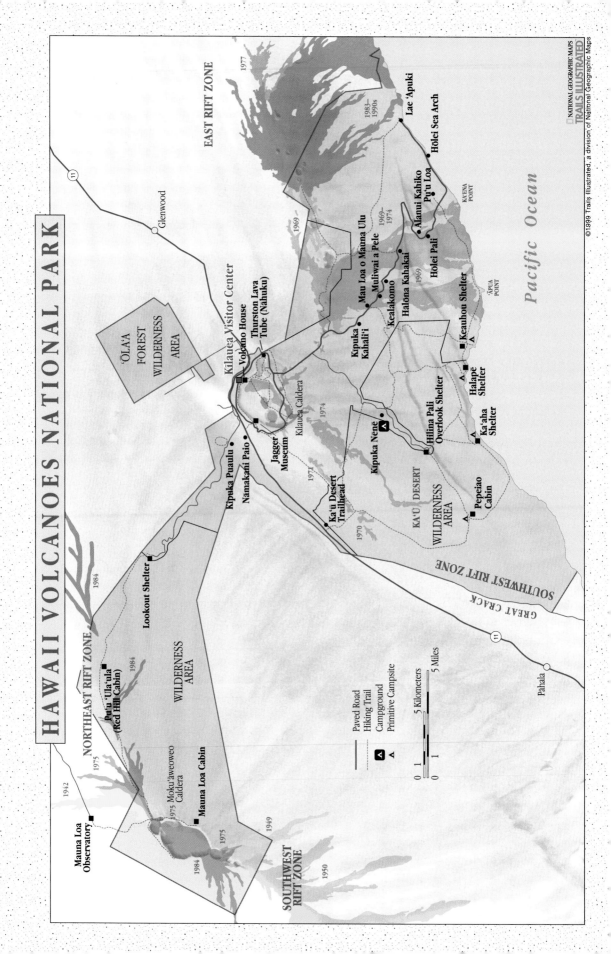

HAWAII VOLCANOES NATIONAL PARK

EAST RIFT ZONE

1977

1983–1990s

Lae 'Apuki

Hōlei Sea Arch

Alanui Kahiko

Pu'u Loa

1969–1974

KA'ENA POINT

Mau Loa o Mauna Ulu

Muliwai a Pele

Hōlei Pali

Kealakomō

1969

Halona Kahakai

'ĀPUA POINT

Keauhou Shelter

Kīpuka Kahali'i

Pacific Ocean

Glenwood

11

1969

Kīlauea Visitor Center

Volcano House

Thurston Lava Tube (Nāhuku)

'ŌLA'A FOREST WILDERNESS AREA

Kīlauea Caldera

Halapē Shelter

Hilina Pali Overlook Shelter

Ka'aha Shelter

Kīpuka Puaulu

Namakani Paio

Jaggar Museum

1974

Kīpuka Nēnē

1974

Ka'ū Desert Trailhead

KA'Ū DESERT WILDERNESS AREA

Pepeiao Cabin

1970

SOUTHWEST RIFT ZONE

GREAT CRACK

11

Pahala

Lookout Shelter

1984

NORTHEAST RIFT ZONE

1975

Pu'u 'Ula'ula (Red Hill Cabin)

1984

WILDERNESS AREA

1942

Moku'āweoweo Caldera

1975

Mauna Loa Cabin

1949

Mauna Loa Observatory

1975

1984

1950

Paved Road
Hiking Trail
Campground
Primitive Campsite

5 Kilometers
5 Miles

0   1
0   1

Hawaii Volcanoes National Park

P.O. Box 52
Hawaii Volcanoes National Park, HI
96718-0052
808-985-6000

This geologically awesome national park displays the results of 70 million years of volcanism and evolution—processes that thrust a bare land from the sea and clothed it with complex and unique ecosystems and a distinct human culture derived from the Polynesian Islands of the South Pacific. Established to protect the natural setting of great mountains of Kilauea and Mauna Loa, the 209,695-acre park is also a refuge for this island's native plants and animals and a link to its human past. Research by scientists at the Hawaiian Volcano Observatory has made Kilauea one of the best understood volcanoes in the world, shedding light on the birth of the Hawaiian Islands and the beginning of planet Earth. In 1916, the park began as part of Hawaii National Park. In 1961, it was established as a separate national park. In 1978, much of the area was designated as wilderness; in 1980, as a Biosphere Reserve; and in 1987, as a World Heritage Site.

As with Haleakala National Park, a rapidly growing problem since the mid-1980s has been the great numbers of helicopter airtour overflights (up to 60 per day over this park!), which create almost constant, substantial, and unacceptable noise that seriously disrupts the natural quiet on the ground. NPCA is strongly urging the implementation of meaningful controls on these flights over Hawaii Volcanoes and Haleakala national parks.

OUTSTANDING FEATURES

Among the many outstanding features of the park are the following: **Mauna Loa**, at 13,677 feet elevation, the world's highest active volcano as well as the most massive mountain on earth, occupying an area of 10,000 cubic miles; **Kilauea Caldera**, at 2 to 2.5 miles across and 500 feet deep in some places, the centerpiece of the park and the location of Halema'uma'u Crater; **Kilauea Rim Rainforest**, a stretch south of the visitor center that has beautiful tree ferns along the rim drive; **Thurston Lava Tube**, which was formed when the exterior of a lava flow cooled to a crust while the still molten interior lava flowed out; **Kilauea Iki Crater**, a pit crater remembered for lava eruptions in 1959 that included a spectacular 1,900-foot-high fountain of molten lava; **Kipuka Puaulu** (Bird Park), one of Hawaii's richest concentrations of native flora and fauna, mercifully bypassed by recent lava flows; and **Sulphur Banks**, a fascinating area of pure sulphur crystalline deposits.

PRACTICAL INFORMATION

When to Go

The park is open year-round. Temperatures are fairly mild year-round, with averages ranging only from 50 to 75 degrees. Mid-summer is usually the driest time of the year; however, visitors should be prepared for variable weather (that is, cold and rainy as well as hot and dry). Mid-December through mid-April and July through August are peak visitor times. Those wishing to avoid tour-bus crowds should try to view major sites before 11 a.m. or after 3 p.m.

How to Get There

By Car: From Hilo, drive southwest 27 miles on State Route 11. From Kailua-Kona, drive southeast 95 miles on Route 11.

By Air: Hilo International Airport (808-934-5801) is served by Aloha and Hawaiian Airlines. Keahole Airport (808-329-2484) just north of Kailua-Kona, is served by Aloha, Hawaiian, and United Airlines.

By Bus: Hele On Bus Company provides service to the park from Hilo once a day on weekdays.

▲ Holei Sea Arch, Hawaii Volcanoes National Park, Hawaii

Fees and Permits

Entrance fees are $10 per vehicle and $5 per person for walk-ins or bicyclists, valid for seven consecutive days. Free backcountry permits are required and are available at the Kilauea Visitor Center.

Visitor Center and Museum

Kilauea Visitor Center: Open daily 7:45 a.m.-5 p.m. Exciting film of volcanic eruptions, interpretive exhibits, publications, maps, video-tapes, and backcountry permits.

Thomas A. Jaggar Museum: Open daily 8:30 a.m.-5 p.m. Outstanding interpretive exhibits on mythology of and scientific research on volcanoes, seismographs and film-strips of current and previous eruptions, publications, and overlooks.

In addition, the Volcano Art Center Gallery features the works of local artists for sale.

Facilities

Marked trails, bookstores, gift shop, drinking water, post office, chapel, and phones.

Handicapped Accessibility

The Kilauea Visitor Center, Jaggar Museum, Volcano House Hotel, and Volcano Art Center are accessible. Pullouts along Crater Rim Drive and Chain of Craters Road afford panoramic views of the park. Accessible pathways include Steam Vents, Keanakako'i, Pu'u Pua'i (Devastation Trail), Pauahi Crater, Muliwai a Pele, Kealakomo, and the Crater Rim Trail along Waldron Ledge. Namakani Paio camp-ground has accessible restrooms and moder-ately accessible campsites. For information on access to park programs, inquire at the Kilauea Visitor Center.

Medical Services

First aid is available at the Kilauea Visitor Center. The closest hospitals from the visitor center are 27 miles to Hilo and 34 miles to Pahala.

Pets

Pets are allowed on leashes not to exceed six feet. They are not permitted in the backcountry, on trails, or in the Kipuka Nene campground. The nearest kennel is in Hilo, 30 miles away. Note that there is a lengthy quarantine period for pets entering Hawaii. Horses, donkeys, and mules are allowed in the backcountry with a valid permit (limit of six animals per site).

Safety and Regulations

For your safety and enjoyment and for the protection of the park, please follow these regulations and suggestions:

- FIRES ARE PROHIBITED, except in the pavilion fireplaces at Namakani Paio, Kipuka Nene, and Kipuka Puaulu. Smoking is not permitted while hiking.

- Park only in designated pullouts, as opposed to grassy areas. Motor vehicles and bicycles must stay on designated roads.

- Park regulations prohibit climbing on or altering rock structures or disturbing or collecting plants, animals, or cultural objects.

This park, situated on two active volcanoes, contains special hidden hazards that may be life-threatening. Follow these recommendations to avoid any problems:

- STAY ON MARKED TRAILS.

- Protect yourself from the heat and intense sunshine, and carry and drink plenty of fluids. Remember that lava fields offer no shade in the hot sun.

- Remember that volcanic fumes are hazardous to your health, especially to young children, pregnant women, and persons with breathing and heart problems. Be alert for indications of sudden danger. Check at the visitor center for volcanic activity and lava-flow viewing opportunities.

- Because the high mountain areas of the park are often cool, rainy, and breezy, hikers should wear sturdy hiking shoes and be prepared for a variety of weather, with clothing for hot, cool, and wet conditions.

- Along the coast, visitors should be extremely careful near steep coastal cliffs and dangerous and unpredictable surf and should be prepared for strong winds.

ACTIVITIES

Hiking, volcano watching, birdwatching, auto tours, nature walks and talks, evening interpretive programs, workshops, seminars, museum exhibits, picnicking, camping, special events, and occasional local entertainment. For an eruption update, call 808-967-7977.

Hiking Trails

The park provides more than 150 miles of hiking trails, including the following: **Thurston Lava Tube Trail** is a short, easy loop that begins at the Crater Rim Drive in a lush rainforest and enters the lava tube. It can also be reached from Volcano House Hotel on a 2.2-mile segment of the Crater Rim Trail; **Kilauea Iki Trail** is a four-mile hike that starts at the Crater Rim Drive, leads around part of the rim, and descends 400 feet into this crater pit that erupted most recently in 1959; **Devastation Trail** is a half-mile excursion from the Crater Rim Drive across a fascinating area of forest that is slowly recovering after the 1959 eruption; **Kipuka Puaulu Trail** is a wonderful one-mile loop that begins near the start of the Moana Loa Strip Road and meanders through one of the park's ecologically richest places; **Napua Trail** leads from the Chain of Craters Road into the East Rift Zone and provides an excellent view of some of the zone's features from atop Pu'u Huluhulu, just a mile from the trailhead; **Pu'u Loa Petroglyphs Trail**, from the Chain of Craters Road, leads .7 mile to an area containing 15,000 petroglyph images carved into the lava rock; and **Puna Coast Trail**, Moana Loa Trail, and others lead hikers through the park's wilderness backcountry.

Scenic Drives

For beautiful views while driving, consider the following: **Crater Rim Drive** is an 11-mile road encircling Kilauea that provides spectacular viewing places of the caldera and other geologic features, passes through lush rainforest and contrastingly arid landscapes, and offers many starting points for hikes; **Chain of Craters Road** is a 20-mile route between Crater Rim Drive and the coast. It follows near Kilauea's East Rift Zone and provides views of craters, along with expanses of lava flows dating from the 1970s, still-active vents along the rift zone, and coastal views. The road ends abruptly where lava flows from 1986 to 1995 obliterated a few miles of the road and other park facilities; and **Mauna Loa Strip Road** is a 13.5-mile drive that leads through an ecologically rich upland forest at Kipuka Puaulu and ends at a Moana Loa lookout point.

OVERNIGHT STAYS

Lodging and Dining

Options include:

The Volcano House Hotel, offering rooms year-round, restaurant, snack shop, bar, gift shops, and outstanding views of Kilauea Caldera.

Kamakani Paio Cabins, offering cabins year-round, picnic tables, and barbecue grills.

For reservations and information about these facilities, contact Volcano House, P.O. Box 53, Hawaii Volcanoes National Park, HI 96718; 808-967-7321.

The nearby communities of Volcano and Hilo also offer a number of motels, bed and breakfasts, and other overnight lodgings.

Campgrounds

Sites in the park's two drive-in campgrounds are open year-round on a first-come, first-served basis. Stays are limited to seven days per year at each campground.

Backcountry Camping

Backcountry camping is allowed year-round at four primitive sites on a first-come, first-served basis. A free permit is required and can be obtained at the Kilauea Visitor Center no earlier than the day before your hike. When you return, check out at the visitor center or call 808-967-7311. Each party of backcountry campers is limited to 12 people, and stays are limited to seven nights per site. Fires are prohibited because of highly flammable grasses and brush.

FLORA AND FAUNA (Partial Listings)

Mammals: Asian mongoose, Hawaiian hoary bat, Hawaiian monk seal, spinner dolphin, and humpback whale.

Birds: white-tailed tropicbird, nene (Hawaiian goose), 'io (Hawaiian hawk), Kalij pheasant, Pacific golden plover, pueo (Hawaiian owl), 'elepaio (Hawaiian flycatcher), 'oma'o (Hawaiian thrush), melodious laughing-thrush, red-billed leiothrix, common myna, Japanese white-eye, northern cardinal, house finch, amakihi, 'i'iwi, 'apapane, and nutmeg mannikin.

Trees, Shrubs, and Flowers: 'ohi'a (an upland tree with scarlet pom-pon-like blossoms), koa (an acacia tree), sandalwood, ti, coconut palm, hapu'u (tree fern), firetree, mamane (palila tree), haha (tree lobelia); shrubs including 'ohelo, pukiawe, mamaki, naupaka, and pilo; and pa'iniu (a rainforest lily that sometimes grows on tree branches).

NEARBY POINTS OF INTEREST

The areas surrounding Hawaii Volcanoes National Park offer a number of fascinating natural and historical attractions that can be enjoyed as day drives or overnight excursions. Akaka Falls State Park, a magnificent 442-foot waterfall viewed from a half-mile paved loop trail through a beautiful area of lush rainforest, is at the end of the spur road (State Route 220) from Honomu, about ten miles from Hilo. Also on the Big Island of Hawaii are Kaloko-Honokohau National Historical Park, Pu'uhonua o Hōnaunau National Historical Park, and Puukohola Heiau National Historic Site. Across the channel on Maui is Haleakala National Park.

JOSHUA TREE NATIONAL PARK

▲ A Joshua tree in flower

JOSHUA TREE NATIONAL PARK

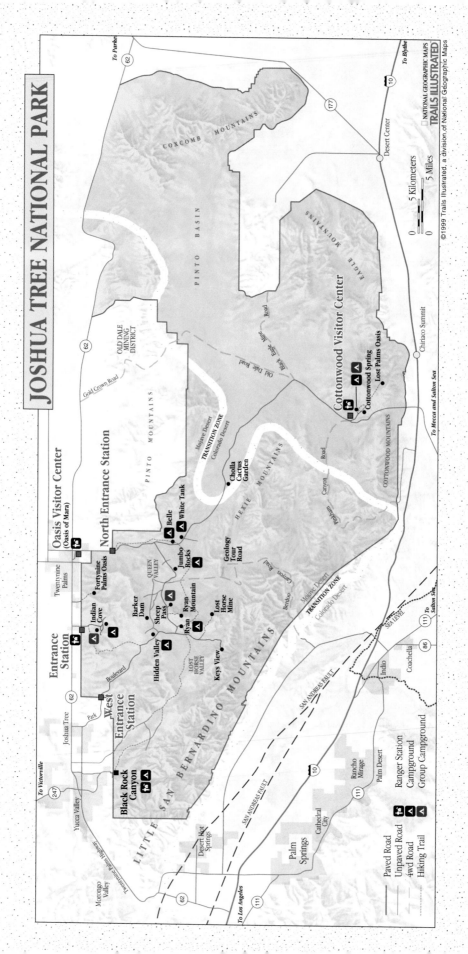

©1999 Trails Illustrated, a division of National Geographic Maps

NATIONAL GEOGRAPHIC MAPS
TRAILS ILLUSTRATED

5 Kilometers
5 Miles

Paved Road
Unpaved Road
4wd Road
Hiking Trail

Ranger Station
Campground
Group Campground

COXCOMB MOUNTAINS

PINTO BASIN

EAGLE MOUNTAINS

Cottonwood Visitor Center

Cottonwood Spring
Lost Palms Oasis

Chiriaco Summit

To Mecca and Salton Sea

Old Dale Mining District

Gold Crown Road

PINTO MOUNTAINS

Old Dale Road

Black Eagle Mine Road

HEXIE MOUNTAINS

Cholla Cactus Garden

Mojave Desert
TRANSITION ZONE
Colorado Desert

Belle
White Tank

Jumbo Rocks

Geology Tour Road

COTTONWOOD MOUNTAINS

Pinkham Canyon Road

Fried Liver Wash Road

Berdoo Canyon Road

Mojave Desert
TRANSITION ZONE
Colorado Desert

Oasis Visitor Center
(Oasis of Mara)

North Entrance Station

Twentynine Palms

Fortynine Palms Oasis

Indian Cove

QUEEN VALLEY

Barker Dam
Sheep Pass
Ryan Mountain
Ryan
Lost Horse Mine

Hidden Valley

LOST HORSE VALLEY

Keys View

Entrance Station

Park Boulevard

West Entrance Station

Joshua Tree

62

SAN BERNARDINO MOUNTAINS

LITTLE SAN BERNARDINO MOUNTAINS

SAN ANDREAS FAULT

SAN ANDREAS FAULT

SEA LEVEL

Black Rock Canyon

Yucca Valley

To Victorville

247

Twentynine Palms Highway

Morongo Valley

To Los Angeles

Desert Hot Springs

Palm Springs

Cathedral City

Rancho Mirage

Palm Desert

Coachella

Indio

SEA LEVEL

111

86

10

111

62

To Parker

62

177

Desert Center

To Blythe

10

Joshua Tree National Park

74485 National Park Drive
Twentynine Palms, CA 92277-3597
760-367-5500

This 792,749-acre national park protects a magnificent, ecologically and scenically diverse area east of Los Angeles, where two major desert regions meet. The Mojave Desert, or high desert, in much of the western and northernmost part of the park, features areas of beautiful, weather-sculpted boulders and rock formations with open stands of the weirdly shaped Joshua tree—a branching, tree-sized variety of yucca. The Colorado Desert, or low desert, in much of the eastern part of the park, is hotter, more arid, and generally more sparsely vegetated; flora includes expanses of the widely spaced creosote bush and such species as teddy bear cactus and ocotillo typical of the Sonoran Desert of southern Arizona. The park also has five delightfully shady spring-fed oases where the native California fan palm grows at the northern limit of its range. The Little San Bernardino Mountains extend through the southwestern part of the park, while Eagle Mountain and the Coxcombs Mountains rise to the east. Following adequate winter rains, the park explodes with incredible carpets of spring wildflowers in virtually every color of the rainbow. Elevations range from 1,900 to 5,100 feet.

In 1936, Joshua Tree was established as a national monument by presidential proclamation. In 1976, much of the monument was designated as wilderness, and in 1984, it was named a Biosphere Reserve. Under the California Desert Protection Act of 1994, the area was enlarged and established as a national park.

OUTSTANDING FEATURES

Among the many outstanding features of the park are the following: stands of the **Joshua tree** (*Yucca brevifolia*), a member of the lily family and the park's namesake, standing with upstretched branches—the largest trees reaching 40 feet in height; **Wonderland of Rocks (Hidden Valley, Queen Valley,** and **Lost Horse Valley)** and **Jumbo Rocks**, magnificently scenic areas of monzogranitic rock formations with Joshua trees scattered picturesquely among them; **Hidden Valley**, a late 19th- and early 20th-century natural corral where rustlers held and re-branded stolen cattle; **Keys View**, a 5,185-foot elevation that on a clear day offers a grand view southward of the Coachella Valley, Mount San Jacinto, the Salton Sea, the Santa Rosa and Chocolate mountains, and even into Mexico, beyond the Imperial Valley; historic **Desert Queen Ranch**, built in 1917 by Bill and Frances Key (with guided tours); **Cholla Cactus Garden**, a dense stand of teddy bear cactus (Bigelow cholla) in Pinto Basin; **Ocotillo Patch**, a dense stand of the tall-stalked, spiny ocotillo; **Cottonwood Spring**, an oasis where early homesteaders or miners planted palms and cottonwood trees, producing a mecca for birdlife; and **Lost Palms Oasis**, the largest natural grove of palms in the park.

PRACTICAL INFORMATION

When to Go

The park is open year-round. Wildflowers bloom mainly in the spring, sometimes beginning as early as February in the low desert and peaking in April at higher elevations. Some annuals bloom into the summer season, which brings intense heat and dryness. Rain usually occurs intermittently throughout the winter, when temperatures remain generally mild and pleasant. In any season, because of the arid desert climate, temperature drops of 40 degrees in a 24-hour period are common.

How to Get There

By Car: From State Route 62, drive south into the park from either Twentynine Palms or Joshua Tree. From I-10, drive north into the park from the Joshua Tree National Park exit (24 miles east of Indio and 24 miles west of Desert Center).

By Air: Palm Springs Municipal Airport (619-323-8161) is served by many domestic airlines.

By Train: Amtrak (800-872-7245) stops in Indio.

By Bus: Morongo Basin Transit Authority (619-367-7433) makes one daily roundtrip from 29 Palms Highway to the Greyhound Station (800-231-2222).

Fees and Permits

Entrance fees are $10 per vehicle or $5 for visitors on foot, bicycle, or motorcycle. Both are valid for seven consecutive days. For backcountry camping, self-registration is required and may be done at any of 12 backcountry boards located throughout the park.

Visitor Centers

Oasis Visitor Center, in Twentynine Palms, just north of the park's main north entrance: open daily 8 a.m.-4:30 p.m.; closed Christmas Day. Interpretive exhibits, publications, maps, and schedules.

Cottonwood Visitor Center: open daily 8 a.m.-4 p.m.; closed Christmas Day and at other times due to staff shortages. Interpretive exhibits, publications, maps, and schedules.

Facilities

Hiking trails, picnic tables, grills, drinking water (at Oasis and Cottonwood visitor centers and Black Rock and Indian Cove ranger stations only).

Handicapped Accessibility

Oasis Visitor Center and garden, Oasis of Mara loop trail, Cap Rock Nature Trail, and Keys View are all wheelchair accessible. The restrooms at White Tank and Belle campgrounds are also accessible.

Medical Services

First aid is available at visitor centers and ranger stations. The closest hospitals are in Joshua Tree, about two miles north of the park, and in Indio, to the south.

Pets

Pet must be leashed at all times. They are prohibited on trails and beyond 100 yards from any road, campground, or picnic area.

Safety and Regulations

For your safety and enjoyment and for the protection of the park, please follow these regulations and suggestions:

- Be extremely careful when driving or walking in the vicinity of mine workings, and *never* enter abandoned mines.

- Always carry plenty of water—at least one gallon per person per day.

- When hiking or walking, watch where you put your hands and feet, especially in summer when rattlesnakes are active.

- Motor vehicles and bicycles must stay on established roads.

- Remember that it is unlawful to feed, hunt, capture, or disturb wildlife and to remove or damage plants or archaeological and other cultural features.

- Firearms and explosives are prohibited.

- Open fires and firewood collecting are not permitted.

The National Park Service asks that visitors not litter the park. Remember the excellent slogan to "leave only footprints" as a guide to help protect this national park.

ACTIVITIES

Hiking, bicycling, birdwatching, photography, rock climbing, interpretive nature walks and talks, evening campfire programs, picnicking, and camping. Further information is available in the park's newspaper, *Joshua Tree Guide*.

Trails

Many miles of trails offer opportunities to explore fascinating parts of this magnificent park. Among them are: **Oasis of Mara Trail**, a half-mile loop from Oasis Visitor Center, through the shaded oasis of palms and

37

cottonwoods; **Arch Rock Nature Trail**, a one-third-mile self-guided interpretive trail amid beautiful boulders and rock formations; **Hidden Valley Trail**, a 1.25-mile trail that winds through varied rock formations; **Barker Dam Trail**, a one-mile trail to a small 1930s reservoir nestled among beautiful rock formations—one of several dams built to create livestock watering holes and now a source of water for desert bighorn sheep and other wildlife; **Ryan Mountain Trail**, a three-mile hike nearly a thousand feet up to this summit, providing a magnificent view of the Wonderland of Rocks; **Ocotillo Patch Trail**, a short interpretive trail; **Cottonwood Spring Trail**, a short walk to an oasis from Cottonwood Visitor Center; **Lost Palms Oasis Trail**, a fairly strenuous, 7.5-mile round-trip hike from Cottonwood Springs Campground to the park's largest California fan palm oasis in a scenic canyon; and **Cholla Cactus Garden Nature Trail**, a short interpretive path (be sure to keep a safe distance from the barbed spines of the Bigelow cholla or teddy bear cactus, known as "jumping" cholla because of the ease with which a "furry-looking," spine-covered segment can be pulled off this cactus and become attached to the skin or clothing of an unsuspecting visitor).

OVERNIGHT STAYS

Lodging and Dining

No lodging or dining facilities are available within the park. The gateway communities of Twentynine Palms, Joshua Tree, and Yucca Valley offer many lodgings and restaurants.

Campgrounds

Group camping and camping at sites at the Black Rock and Indian Cove campgrounds may be reserved through National Park Reservation Service (800-365-CAMP). All other camp sites in the park are available on a first-come, first-served basis. Horses are allowed at Black Rock Campground. RVs up to 32 feet long are permitted in the campgrounds. Campers must furnish their own water and firewood, and fires are allowed only in grills provided. There is a 14-day limit at all campgrounds from September through May and a 30-day limit from June through August.

Backcountry Camping

Backcountry camping is allowed throughout much of the park on a first-come, first-served basis. The park staff recommends camping in the fall, winter, or spring because, in the summer, high temperatures are common and there is no water and little respite from the heat. Campsites must be at least one mile from any road, 500 feet from trails, and ¼ mile from any natural or human water source, including springs, seeps, dams, and tanks. Camping is prohibited in day-use areas. Strenuous backpacking requires two gallons of water per person per day. Be advised that water is not available in the backcountry—you must carry enough water (one gallon per person per day) to last the length of your trip.

FLORA AND FAUNA (Partial Listings)

Mammals: desert bighorn sheep, mule deer, bobcat, coyote, gray and kit foxes, badger, black-tailed jack rabbit, desert cottontail, ringtail, spotted and striped skunks, California and round-tailed ground squirrels, Merriam's chipmunk, and wood and kangaroo rats.

Birds: Of the more than 235 species of birds recorded in the park, there are: Gambel's quail, red-tailed hawk, golden eagle, turkey vulture, prairie falcon, kestrel, great horned and screech owls, mourning dove, roadrunner, hummingbirds (Anna's, Costa's, and black-chinned), ladder-backed woodpecker, western kingbird, Say's and black phoebes, white-throated swift, raven, scrub and pinyon jays, mountain chickadee, plain titmouse, bushtit, verdin, wrens (Bewick's, cactus, canyon, and rock), black-tailed and blue-gray gnatcatchers, mockingbird, thrashers (Bendire's, California, and LeConte's), loggerhead shrike, phainopepla, orioles (northern, hooded, and Scott's), western tanager, sparrows (black-chinned, black-throated, sage, and white-crowned),

39

▲ *Joshua tree and granite boulders, Joshua Tree National Park, California*

▲ *Mojave mound cactus/claret cup, Joshua Tree National Park, California*

dark-eyed junco, California and rufous-sided towhees, house finch, and lesser goldfinch.

Amphibians and Reptiles: desert tortoise, California tree frog, red-spotted toad, chuckwalla, desert iguana, lizards (collared, leopard, desert night, fringe-toed, western whiptail, and side-blotched), striped racer, rosy boa, and rattlesnakes (sidewinder, speckled, and Mojave).

Trees, Shrubs, Flowers, and Ferns: single-leaf pinyon, California juniper, willow, Turbinella scrub and canyon live oaks, cottonwood, smoke tree, California fan palm, Joshua tree, Mojave yucca, Parry nolina, ocotillo, mesquite, manzanita, chuparosa, creosote bush, brittlebush, desert mariposa lily, alyssum, amaranth, globemallow, bladderpod, blue lupine, Canterbury bells, wooly marigold, evening primrose, sand verbena, desert dandelion, desert gold poppy, chia, phacelia, fiddleneck, sacred datura, scarlet locoweed, filaree, forget-me-not, helleborine orchid, Indian paintbrush, Mojave aster, desert sunflower, maidenhair fern, and a number of cacti, including barrel, old man, Calico hedgehog, beavertail prickly pear, and Mojave mound.

NEARBY POINTS OF INTEREST

The areas surrounding Joshua Tree National Park offer many fascinating natural attractions that can be enjoyed as day trips or overnight excursions. The half-million-acre Anza-Borrego Desert State Park to the south encompasses a large expanse of the Colorado Desert—including the erosion-sculpted, undulating and rippled maze of the Borrego Badlands, shady Borrego Palm Canyon, and Split Mountain Canyon, near which grows the strange-looking elephant tree. To the west of Joshua Tree National Park are the San Bernardino and Angeles national forests in the rugged San Bernardino and San Gabriel mountains. To the southwest is the Mount San Jacinto unit of San Bernardino National Forest, surrounding spectacular Mount San Jacinto State Park that protects the heights around this 10,786-foot-high summit. Death Valley National Park is to the north of Joshua Tree. To the northeast lies Mojave National Preserve. Several important U.S. Bureau of Land Management areas are also near the park: Big Morongo Preserve, Mecca Hills Recreation Area, and Coachella Valley Preserve.

Lassen Volcanic National Park

▲ View from ridge above Blue Lake Canyon

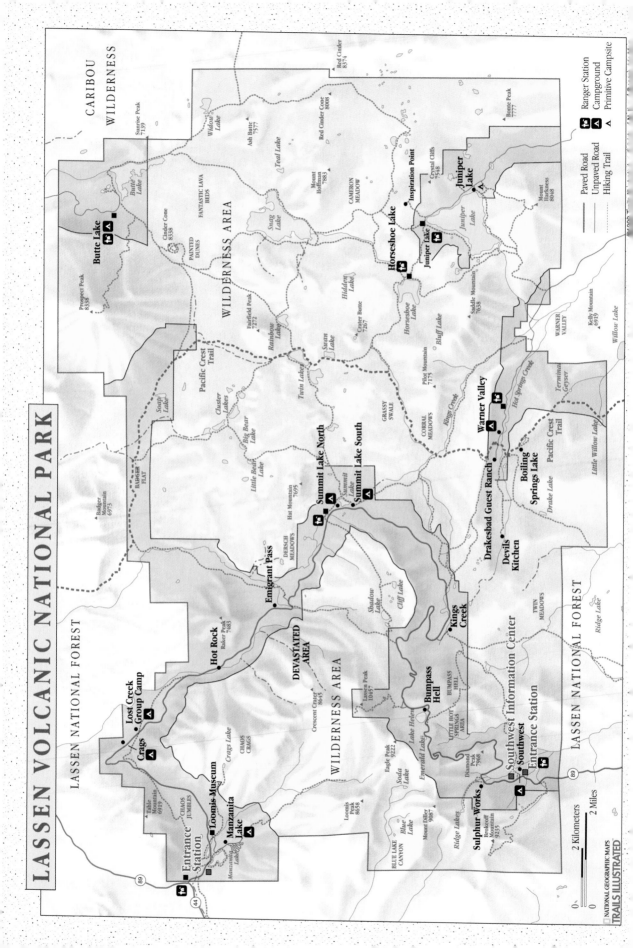

Lassen Volcanic National Park

P.O. Box 100
Mineral, CA 96063-0100
530-595-4444

Established for its significance as a recently active volcanic landscape, this 106,372-acre national park in northern California is a virtual research laboratory of volcanic phenomena and associated geothermal features. The mountain's most recent major activity occurred in 1914 and 1915, with more than 150 eruptions of ash, gases, and steam, causing horrendous devastation including an immense flood of mud that roared down the slopes, laying waste to everything in its way. The volcano's billowing cloud at the time spewed from deep within the earth to at least 30,000 feet. Since a small eruption that followed in 1921, it has been dormant.

The great mountain is part of a vast geographic unit—a great lava plateau with isolated volcanic peaks—that also encompasses Lava Beds National Monument and Crater Lake National Park in Oregon. The park features great lava pinnacles, huge mountains created by lava flows, jagged craters, steaming sulphur vents, cinder cones, hot springs, sparkling lakes, and dashing mountain streams. Spectacular glaciated canyons, year-round snowbanks, and meadows of wildflowers highlight the landscape, some of which is forested largely with conifers. Here visitors can see firsthand how explosively powerful volcanic forces deep within the earth can suddenly transform the landscape and lead to the creation of a beautiful wilderness ecosystem. In 1907, the site was established by presidential proclamation as Lassen Peak and Cinder Cone national monuments. In 1916, these two areas became part of Lassen Volcanic National Park, and in 1972 much of the park was designated as wilderness.

OUTSTANDING FEATURES

Among the many outstanding features of the park are the following: **Lassen Peak**, the world's largest plug-dome volcano, rising to 10,457 feet; **Lake Helen**, a beautiful lake with a close-up view of the peak; **Reflection Lake**, which offers a pine-framed view of the peak and **Chaos Jumbles**, a large rock avalanche that fell about 300 years ago; **Cinder Cone**, a nearly symmetrical, 755-foot mound of lava surrounded by multicolored cinders; **Sulphur Works**, a thermal-spring area containing fumaroles, boiling mud pots, and hot springs; **Bumpass Hell**, the largest and most spectacular thermal-spring area in the park; and the **Devastated Area**, scarred land from the massive eruption in May 1915.

PRACTICAL INFORMATION

When to Go

The park is open year-round. The volcanic areas can be visited in the spring through fall, and restrooms other than the Chalet restroom are open only in summer. Summer is pleasant, with temperatures in the 70s and 80s. Heavy, persistent rains over periods of seven to ten days may be experienced in winter, when average daily temperatures are between 20 and 50 degrees. Snowfall can be heavy throughout winter months.

How to Get There

By Car: From I-5 at Red Bluff, drive east two miles on State Route 99, east 45 miles on State Route 36, and north about five miles on State Route 89 to the park's southwest entrance. From I-5 at Redding, drive east 47 miles on State Route 44 to the park's north entrance. From Susanville, drive northwest 65 miles on State Route 44 to the park's north entrance. The Drakesbad area of the park is reached from State Route 36 at Chester, northwest a few miles to the southeast entrance to the park.

By Air: Airlines serve Redding, Reno, and Chico airports.

By Train: Amtak (800-372-7245) stops in Redding and Chico.

By Bus: Greyhound Lines (800-231-2222) stops in Red Bluff and Redding. Mount Lassen Motor Transit stops in Mineral and Red Bluff, Mondays through Saturdays.

Fees and Permits

Entrance fee is $10 per vehicle or $5 for visitors on foot, bicycle, motorcycle, or by bus. Fees are valid for seven consecutive days. Backcountry permits are required and available at park headquarters, Loomis Museum, and all ranger stations. Request them by mail at least two weeks in advance.

A state fishing license is required. Emerald Lake, Manzanita Creek, and 150 feet from the Manzanita Lake inlet are closed to fishing. Special regulations for Manzanita Lake: catch and release only; with artificial lures and single barbless hooks only.

Information Stations and Museum

Southwest Information Station: open Fridays through Mondays, from June through Labor Day. Information, publications, maps, and schedules.

Park Headquarters: open daily 8 a.m.-4:30 p.m., from Memorial Day to Labor Day. Publications, permits, information, maps, and schedules.

Loomis Museum: open daily 9 a.m.-5 p.m., from mid-June to early September. Interpretive exhibits, audiovisual programs, publications, maps, permits, and schedules.

Facilities

Hiking trails, boat launch, cross-country ski trails, picnic facilities, equipment rentals, cafe, gift shops, camping supplies, service station, propane, groceries, hot showers, laundry, and fishing tackle.

Handicapped Accessibility

Loomis Museum, Camper Store, Manzanita Lake Campground, Summit Lake Campground, Southwest Campground, Park Headquarters,

Devastated Area Nature Trail, and several naturalist programs are wheelchair accessible.

Medical Services

First aid is available at the Loomis Museum and ranger stations. Hospitals are in Red Bluff, Redding, Burney, Susanville, and Chester.

Pets

Pets must remain leashed or otherwise physically restrained at all times. They are not permitted on trails, in the backcountry, in buildings, at evening talks, or in any body of water.

Safety and Regulations

For your safety and enjoyment and for the protection of the park, please follow these regulations and suggestions:

- Because boiling water and scalding mud may be present at or near the ground surface in park thermal areas, the National Park Service warns visitors to stay on trails and boardwalks, keep alert for possible danger, and maintain close control over young children.

- Avoid exposed terrain during lightning storms.

- Remember that volcanic rock is generally unstable and poorly suited to rock climbing.

- Motorized vehicles and bicycles must stay on established roads.

- Motorized boats are prohibited on all park waters. Emerald, Reflection, and Boiling Springs lakes and Lake Helen are closed to boating. At other lakes, boaters are required to use only the designated launch sites. Boats may not be left overnight on lake shores.

ACTIVITIES

Hiking, birdwatching, swimming, fishing, boating (no motors), cross-country skiing and snowshoeing, nature walks and talks, evening campfire programs, children's activities, picnicking, and camping. Further information is available in the park's newspaper, *Lassen Park Guide*.

▲ *Lassen Volcanic National Park, California*

Hiking Trails

The park provides 150 miles of trails, a few of which are the following: **Sulphur Works Trail**, a short self-guided trail through a geothermal area of bubbling hot springs and steaming fumaroles; **Bumpass Hell Trail**, a three-mile interpretive hike leading through a fascinating landscape of boiling, bubbling, and steaming hot springs, fumaroles, and mud pots; **Lassen Peak Trail**, a very strenuous, 2.5-mile trail, 2,000-foot climb to the 10,457-foot-high summit (hikers should be physically fit and acclimatized before making this climb); **Devastated Area Trail**, an area showing the slow recovery of vegetation since the devastating impact of the 20-foot-high mud flow that roared down the mountainside in 1915; **Manzanita and Reflection Lakes Trail**, loops around the shores of these lakes that provide opportunities to enjoy views of Lassen Peak and Chaos Jumbles reflected on their surface; **Manzanita Creek Trail**, a hike that climbs for about four miles across sunny, open expanses of manzanita, through shady stands

of tall firs and beautiful Jeffrey pines, and then follows a stretch of dashing Manzanita Creek, along which tiny yellow violet flowers bloom in June; **Cinder Cone Trail**, in the northeast corner of the park, which leads 2.5 miles from the campground near the shore of Butte Lake and climbs to the summit of this 750-foot-high cone of black cinders; and the **Pacific Coast Trail**, winding north-south through the park's wilderness backcountry.

OVERNIGHT STAYS

Lodging and Dining

Options include:

Drakesbad Guest Ranch, offering lodge rooms, cabins, and bungalows from mid-June through September. Meals, swimming pool, and horseback riding. Reservations are recommended; call the long distance operator, ask for the Susanville, California, operator, then ask for Drakesbad Toll Station #2.

Lassen Chalet Cafe, offering breakfast and lunch daily, dinners during July and August, and outside deck dining, weather permitting.

For more information on these facilities, contact California Guest Services, Inc., 2150 Main Street, Suite 5, Red Bluff, CA 96080; 916-529-1512:

Lodging and dining facilities are also available in Mineral, Hat Creek, and other communities in the vicinity of the park.

Campgrounds

Campgrounds are open from about Memorial Day weekend through most of September; exact dates depend upon road and weather conditions. All sites are available on a first-come, first-served basis. Reservations for group camping are made by contacting the park. Group sites are for organized groups only, and each site accommodates up to 25 people. Campers should keep a clean campsite and properly store food to avoid attracting black bears.

Backcountry Camping

Camping in the wilderness backcountry is allowed all year throughout much of the park on a first-come, first-served basis. Free permits are required and are available at least two weeks in advance from park information stations, entrance stations, the Loomis Museum, and ranger stations. To request a permit by mail, call park headquarters. Fires are prohibited in the backcountry. Camp at least one mile from developed areas, campgrounds, or park roads.

FLORA AND FAUNA (Partial Listings)

Mammals: black bear, blacktail (mule) deer, mountain lion, bobcat, coyote, red and gray foxes, badger, yellow-bellied marmot, beaver, muskrat, pine marten, mink, long-tailed weasel, mountain beaver, porcupine, spotted and striped skunks, raccoon, river otter, snowshoe hare, Nuttall's cottontail, pika, Douglas' and gray squirrels, squirrels (golden-mantled, Belding's, and California ground), chipmunks (Townsend's, lodgepole, and yellow pine).

Birds: pied-billed grebe, Canada goose, mallard, common merganser, coot, killdeer, spotted sandpiper, blue grouse, mountain quail, red-tailed hawk, golden eagle, kestrel, pygmy and great horned owl, calliope hummingbird, woodpeckers (pileated, white-headed, hairy, and three-toed), flicker, red-breasted sapsucker, olive-sided flycatcher, western wood-pewee, Steller's jay, Clark's nutcracker, mountain chickadee, nuthatches (white-breasted, red-breasted, and pygmy), brown creeper, winter wren, dipper, ruby- and golden-crowned kinglets, robin, Townsend's solitaire, warblers (yellow-rumped, hermit, black-throated gray, MacGillivray's, yellow, orange-crowned, and Wilson's), western tanager, hermit thrush, sparrows (white-crowned, chipping, fox, song, and Lincoln's), dark-eyed junco, black-headed grosbeak, finches (gray-crowned rosy, purple, and Cassin's), and evening grosbeak.

Trees, Shrubs, and Flowers: pines (western white, sugar, lodgepole, ponderosa, and Jeffrey), mountain hemlock, white and red firs, incense cedar, quaking aspen, bush chinkapin, manzanita, ceanothus, gooseberry, arrowleaf balsamroot, blue-eyed grass, Brewer Mountain heath, buckwheat, camas lily, dwarf hulsea, Fremont groundsel, giant coreopsis, spotted coralroot, pyrola, Indian paintbrush, iris, lupine, skunk-leaf polemonium, monkeyflower, monkshood, columbine, oxalis, pentstemon, phacelia, rock spirea, golden draba, snow plant, and violet.

NEARBY POINTS OF INTEREST

The area surrounding Lassen Volcanic National Park offers many fascinating natural attractions that can be enjoyed as day trips or overnight excursions. The park is surrounded by the Lassen National Forest. About 70 miles due north of the park is Lava Beds National Monument and the adjacent Tule Lake National Wildlife Refuge. The National Park Service-managed Whiskeytown Unit of the Whiskeytown-Shasta-Trinity National Recreation Area is about 60 miles to the west. The U.S. Bureau of Land Management-administered Eagle Lake, Bizz Johnson Trail, and Biscar Wildlife Refuge are also located near the park.

MOJAVE NATIONAL PRESERVE

▲ Mojave yucca, Granite Mountains

Mojave National Preserve

P.O. Box 241
Baker, CA 92309
760-733-4040

In 1994, the California Desert Protection Act established the 1,450,000-acre Mojave National Preserve, in the heart of the Mojave Desert of southeastern California, to protect this area's fascinating natural and cultural values. It is a magnificent expanse of ecologically and geologically significant desert valleys, basins, bajadas, and upthrusting fault-block and volcanic mountains, with such features as the second-tallest sand dunes in the United States, volcanic cinder cones and lava flows, areas of weather-sculpted rock formations, the largest expanse anywhere of Joshua trees (Yucca brevifolia), an abundance of historic sites, and a remarkable diversity and abundance of flora and fauna. More than 700 species of plantlife, at least 200 kinds of birds, more than 50 species of mammals, and numerous varieties of reptiles have been recorded here.

In 1981, the area was initially designated by the U.S. Department of the Interior as the East Mojave National Scenic Area, under the Bureau of Land Management. NPCA had recommended this designation as a first step toward enhanced protective management of this magnificently scenic and ecologically fragile area. However, after a few years, a coalition of environmental organizations, including NPCA, became convinced that truly adequate protection from extractive resource uses, target shooting, off-road vehicle events, and other harmful activities could come about only with the area's transfer to the National Park Service. Following intensive efforts over a period of eight years, Congress finally established the national preserve, parts of which were simultaneously designated as wilderness.

OUTSTANDING FEATURES

Among the many outstanding features of the park are the following: **Kelso Sand Dunes**, the second tallest dunes in the United States, rising to 700 feet; the ruggedly scenic **Granite-South Providence-Providence-New York Mountains**, which run like a huge upthrusted backbone from southwest to northeast through the preserve; **Cima Dome**, an extensive upwarped hump of land, whose gently rounded topography rises 1,500 feet and extends across nearly 50,000 acres; **Devil's Playground** and **Soda Dry Lake**, the latter a vast playa where a lake existed once, during a wetter period of earth history; **Clark Mountain**, at 7,929 feet elevation, the highest peak in the preserve, where there is a small relic stand of white fir; **Piute Gorge**, a spectacular sheer gorge that is nearly 200 feet deep; **Piute Creek**, an area that provides one of the very few riparian habitats in the preserve; **Camp Rock Spring**, one of the most isolated U.S. Army posts in the history of the West, providing escorts for the U.S. Mail and protection for travelers; **Camp Ibis**, one of 11 World War II training center camps in the desert of Arizona and California under the command of General George S. Patton; **Sheep Corral**, at the base of the Granite Mountains, a scenic gem of a little valley of rounded monzonite rock formations cut by a maze of usually dry washes; **Hole-in-the-Wall**, featuring colorful rhyolite rock formations of volcanic origin—a place of intriguing beauty where visitors occasionally see desert bighorn sheep; and **Carruthers Canyon** and **Fourth of July Canyon**, in the New York Mountains, which provide ecologically important habitat for a great variety of flora and fauna, including species of coastal chaparral and live oaks that seem removed from their normal range, far inland and surrounded by the desert.

ACTIVITIES

Hiking, birdwatching, photography, auto tours, bicycling, hunting in some areas, interpretive nature walks and programs, picnicking, and camping. Further information is available in the park's newspaper, Mojave National Preserve.

When to Go

The preserve is open year-round. The best months for visiting are October through May since summer daytime temperatures average more than 100 degrees. Interpretive programs are offered in the spring (especially in late March, April, and early May after winters of sufficient rainfall), when wildflowers spread across the desert. Average temperatures in spring and fall range from about 55 to 80 degrees; in winter, from about 40 to 60 degrees. Because of the desert's extremely low humidity, nights can be quite cool to cold in every season.

How to Get There

By Car: From Barstow, California, drive northeast 60 miles on I-15, or from Las Vegas, Nevada, southeast 90 miles on I-15, to the Baker exit, and south into the preserve on the Kelbaker Road. Among other exits into the preserve from I-15: at 26 miles northeast of Baker, and south into the preserve. From Barstow, you can also drive east 80 miles on I-40, or from Needles, California, west 60 miles on I-40, to the national preserve exit, and north into the preserve. Other exits from I-40 include the road to the Providence Mountains State Recreation Area (within the preserve), east 115 miles from Barstow. From Death Valley National Park, the preserve is reached south on State Route 127 to Baker, across the I-15 overpass, and into the preserve on the Kelbaker Road.

By Air: McCarran International Airport (702-261-5743) in Las Vegas is served by most major airlines.

By Train: Amtrak (800-872-7245) stops in Barstow and Las Vegas.

By Bus: Greyhound Lines (800-231-2222) stops in Barstow and Las Vegas.

Fees and Permits

There is no entrance fee, but fees are charged for camping.

Information and Visitor Centers

Mojave National Preserve Information Center, located in Baker: Open daily year-round. Information and schedules.

Hole-in-the-Wall Visitor Center: Open daily from November through April. Information, publications, maps, spring interpretive programs, and schedules.

Facilities

Limited drinking water, two developed trails, general store and post office, picnic tables, restrooms, campgrounds.

Handicapped Accessibility

The Hole-in-the-Wall Visitor Center and all sites at the nearby campground are wheelchair accessible. Most information is available in print, and all park programs can be altered for specific needs; contact the park for more information.

Medical Services

First aid is available at the Hole-in-the-Wall Visitor Center and from rangers. Hospitals are in Las Vegas, Barstow, and Needles.

Pets

Pets are permitted on leashes not to exceed six feet in length. Visitors should not allow their pets to disturb other visitors or the wildlife and should not leave pets locked in vehicles, a situation that especially in high temperatures can be fatal.

Safety and Regulations

For your safety and enjoyment and for the protection of the park, please follow these regulations and suggestions:

- Because temperatures can be extreme and water scarce, visitors are advised to carry a generous supply of water and, when hiking, to drink at least one gallon per person per day.

- Wear clothing that will protect against the heat of the sun and the wind.

49

▲ *Beavertail cactus, Mojave National Preserve, California*

- Be sure that you and your vehicle are prepared for extreme conditions.

- Be alert for the possibility of flash floods and rattlesnakes, especially the Mojave "green" rattlesnake.

- Because fuel, water, and telephones are widely scattered and many roads crisscross through the preserve, visitors are urged to study good road maps and keep oriented. Hikers are advised to be extremely aware of where they are and not to stray from established trails.

- Hunting is permitted only in designated areas and in accordance with federal, state, and local regulations; target shooting and plinking are not permitted.

- Motor vehicles and bicycles must remain on established roads.

- No open fires or firewood gathering are allowed; fires are permitted only in established grates at campgrounds or in campstoves. Be sure to bring your own firewood and water.

The National Park Service urges visitors to respect privately owned lands that are scattered across parts of the preserve, especially where owners have posted them against trespassing. Livestock grazing is a use permitted in the reserve; consequently, visitors should drive with care since cattle sometimes walk slowly across roads.

OVERNIGHT STAYS

Lodging and Dining

No lodging or dining facilities are available in the preserve. The communities of Baker, Barstow, and Needles offer overnight lodgings and restaurants, and a bed-and-breakfast and cafe are located at Nipton.

Campgrounds

There are two campgrounds in the park: Hole-in-the-Wall Campground, at 4,200 feet in elevation, near beautiful rock formations; and Mid Hills Campground, at 5,600 feet elevation, situated in a pinyon-juniper woodland. (Note that temperatures are usually about 10 to 15 degrees cooler at Mid Hills than at Hole-in-the-Wall.) Both campgrounds provide restrooms, picnic tables, fire rings, and sometimes water. Firewood and hookups are not available, so be sure to bring your own water and firewood.

Roadside camping is also permitted throughout much of the park. Group camping is available by reservation (contact the Hole-in-the-Wall Visitor Center or the California Desert Information Center). An equestrian campground is available in the group campground, and reservations are not required; horses are not permitted in the other campgrounds.

Backcountry Camping

Backcountry camping is allowed all year throughout much of the preserve. Permits are not required. Campsites must be more than one-half mile from a road and more than 1,000 feet from a water source. Please practice minimum-impact camping and pack out all trash. The limit of stay is 14 days per site.

FLORA AND FAUNA (Partial Listings)

Mammals: desert bighorn sheep, mule deer, mountain lion, bobcat, coyote, gray and kit foxes, badger, porcupine, ringtail, spotted skunk, black-tailed jackrabbit, desert cottontail, California and round-tailed ground squirrels, white-tailed antelope squirrel, Panamint chipmunk, and wood and kangaroo rats.

▼*Borrego milkvetch, Mojave National Preserve, California*

Birds: Gambel's and mountain quail, red-tailed hawk, golden eagle, turkey vulture, kestrel, prairie falcon, great horned owl, mourning dove, roadrunner, nighthawk, hummingbirds (poorwill, Costa's, black-chinned, and broad-tailed), flicker, western kingbird, ash-throated flycatcher, Say's phoebe, horned lark, white-throated swift, raven, scrub and pinyon jays, mountain chickadee, plain titmouse, wrens (Bewick's, rock, canyon, and cactus), blue-gray and black-tailed gnatcatchers, mockingbird, LeConte's thrasher, Townsend's solitaire, mountain bluebird, loggerhead shrike, phainopepla, yellow-breasted chat, warblers (yellow-rumped, black-throated gray, yellowthroat, and orange-crowned), great-tailed grackle, western meadowlark, Scott's oriole, western tanager, sparrows (white-crowned, black-throated, and Brewer's), rufous-sided and green-tailed towhees, dark-eyed junco, house finch, and lesser goldfinch.

Reptiles: desert tortoise, chuckwalla, Gila monster, fringe-toed lizard, and the sidewinder and olive-green phase of the Mojave rattlesnake. Visitors should be especially respectful of the latter species, as it has an unusual neurotoxic venom for which there is no known antitoxin.

Trees, Shrubs, and Flowers: Trees include Rocky Mountain white fir, singleleaf and two-needled pinyons, Utah and California junipers, turbinella scrub and canyon live oaks, Fremont cottonwood, Joshua tree, Mohave and banana yuccas, desert agave, desert willow, and smoke-tree. Shrubs include mesquite, catclaw acacia, creosotebush, silk tassel, four-winged saltbush, manzanita, California lilac (ceonothus), Great Basin sagebrush, burrobush, cheesebush, desert almond, blackbrush, winter fat, blue and Mojave sages, brittlebush, rabbitbrush, and yerba santa.

Examples of the many wildflowers are desert gold poppy, gold cups, golden gilia, desert marigold, coreopsis, encelia, desert and mariposa lilies, chia, desert larkspur, desert globemallow, dune primrose, prince's plume, tidy tips, wind mills, phacelias, fiddleneck, Indian paintbrush, lilac sunbonnet, Canterbury bells, desert dandelion, tack-stem, giant four-o'clock, locoweed, purplemat, Palmer and red penstemons, sand verbena, prickly poppy, sacred datura, desert trumpet, and Mojave aster. Of the cacti, there are silver, pencil, and buckhorn chollas, along with beavertail prickly pear, barrel, hedgehog, old man, Mojave mound, and pincushion.

NEARBY POINTS OF INTEREST

The areas surrounding Mojave National Preserve offer a variety of fascinating natural and historical attractions that can be enjoyed as day trips or overnight excursions. Located within the preserve is the Providence Mountains State Recreation Area, featuring Mitchell Caverns. Lake Mead National Recreation Area is directly to the northeast along the Colorado River in Nevada and Arizona. Lake Havasu National Wildlife Refuge is located along the Arizona shore of this Colorado River reservoir, extending southeastward from Lake Havasu City. Death Valley National Park is to the north, and Joshua Tree National Park is to the southwest.

The U.S. Bureau of Land Management administers the Fort Piute Historic Site and Afton Canyon, located near the preserve, as well as vast areas surrounding the preserve. Rainbow Basin National Natural Landmark is located just to the northwest of Barstow.

REDWOOD NATIONAL PARK

▲ Rhododendrons, Lady Bird Johnson Grove

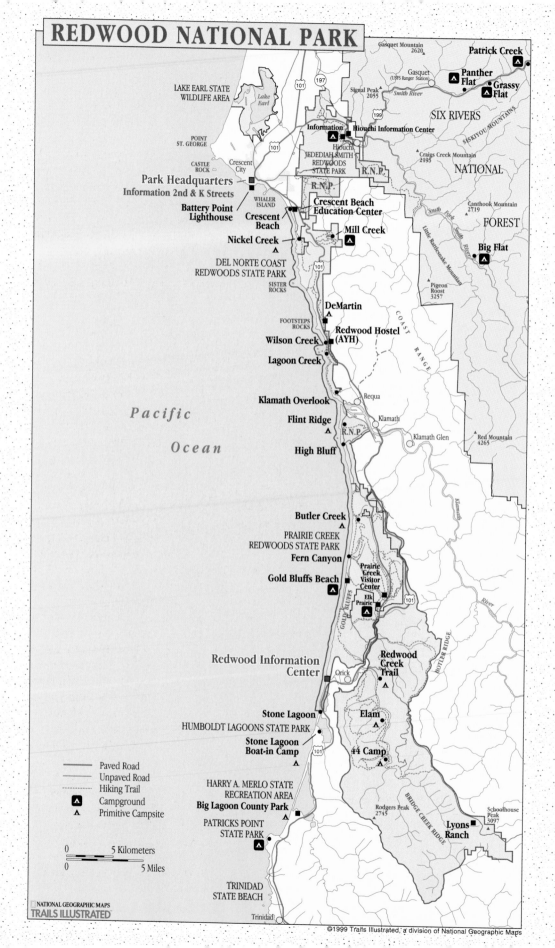

REDWOOD NATIONAL PARK

Gasquet Mountain 2620

Patrick Creek

Panther Flat

Gasquet (USFS Ranger Station)

Grassy Flat

Signal Peak 2055

Smith River

SIX RIVERS

LAKE EARL STATE WILDLIFE AREA

Lake Earl

Craigs Creek Mountain 2195

NATIONAL

Information

Houchi Information Center

Houchi

JEDEDIAH SMITH REDWOODS STATE PARK

R.N.P.

Canthook Mountain 2719

POINT ST. GEORGE

R.N.P.

South Fork

Little Rattlesnake Mountain

FOREST

CASTLE ROCK

Crescent City

Big Flat

Park Headquarters
Information 2nd & K Streets

WHALER ISLAND

Crescent Beach Education Center

Pigeon Roost 3257

Battery Point Lighthouse

Crescent Beach

Mill Creek

Nickel Creek

DEL NORTE COAST REDWOODS STATE PARK

SISTER ROCKS

DeMartin

COAST RANGE

FOOTSTEPS ROCKS

Redwood Hostel (AYH)

Wilson Creek

Lagoon Creek

Requa

Pacific

Klamath Overlook

Klamath

Ocean

Flint Ridge

R.N.P.

Klamath Glen

Red Mountain 4265

High Bluff

Klamath

Butler Creek

PRAIRIE CREEK REDWOODS STATE PARK

Fern Canyon

Prairie Creek Visitor Center

Gold Bluffs Beach

Elk Prairie

GOLD BLUFFS

River

Redwood Creek Trail

HOTLER RIDGE

Redwood Information Center

Orick

Stone Lagoon

Elam

HUMBOLDT LAGOONS STATE PARK

Stone Lagoon Boat-in Camp

44 Camp

HARRY A. MERLO STATE RECREATION AREA

BRIDGE CREEK RIDGE

Big Lagoon County Park

Rodgers Peak 2745

Schoolhouse Peak 3097

PATRICKS POINT STATE PARK

Lyons Ranch

Paved Road
Unpaved Road
Hiking Trail
Campground
Primitive Campsite

0   5 Kilometers
0   5 Miles

TRINIDAD STATE BEACH

Trinidad

REDWOOD NATIONAL PARK

1111 2nd Street
Crescent City, CA 95531-4198
707-464-6101

This 110,232-acre national park, including three state parks, protects magnificent virgin-growth groves of the world's tallest tree species—the towering coast redwoods (*Sequoia sempervirens*). The tallest known redwood, rising 367 feet, is in a creekside grove in Redwood Creek Valley. The oldest of these trees has been living for more than 2,000 years. Often kept cool and damp by summer coastal fog and soaked with frequent winter rains that total between 50 and 100 inches per year, these great trees are part of a rich forest ecosystem. Rhododendrons bloom pink in May; maples turn yellow in autumn; and a wealth of wildflowers, ferns, mosses, lichens, and fungi grow beneath the towering giants. In spring, the magical songs of hermit and varied thrushes and the tiny winter wren break the muffled silence of these awesome cathedral-groves. The park also protects many miles of beautiful streams and 40 miles of ruggedly scenic coastline of bluffs, sheer cliffs and headlands, rocky shore with tidepools, and "seastacks," a broad strand of ocean beach where Roosevelt elk sometimes gather. From sea level to 3,100 feet up in the Coast Range, this mild, damp climate produces habitat for a diversity of wildlife. It is an ideal environment in which the titans of the forest have thrived for hundreds and even thousands of years.

Within the national park boundary are 33,801 acres of Prairie Creek Redwoods, Del Norte Coast Redwoods, and Jedediah Smith Redwoods state parks. The magnificent virgin-growth redwood groves in these three parks, which predate establishment of Redwood National Park, would have been logged off many decades ago except for the timely action of the State of California and generous matching funds from donors throughout the United States to the Save-the-Redwoods League.

With increasing recognition that there should be a national park of the redwoods, Congress in 1968, in the face of heavy oppo-sition from the timber industry, established a Redwood National Park containing 58,000 acres (including the three state parks). The federal holdings centered largely at the lower end of Redwood Creek Valley, with a narrow strip of parkland extending up-valley to include the Tall Tree Grove, containing the world's tallest known tree. Outside the park, however, feverish clear-cut logging on the valley's steep slopes continued to leave in their wake an ecological nightmare of devastated watersheds and massive erosion. Redwoods thought to have been "saved" in the park, including the Tall Tree Grove itself, were threatened with destruction from heavy flooding and siltation. Environmental groups, including NPCA, urged meaningful park expansion.

Fortunately, in 1978, Congress authorized the addition of 48,000 acres—extending the park farther up-valley and from ridge-to-ridge across the valley. About 30,000 acres of this new parkland contained severe logging and erosion damage, much of it created by the 250-mile maze of abandoned logging roads and tractor trails. Since then, a major watershed and landscape rehabilitation program has been undertaken by the National Park Service to help restore the shattered ecosystem. This ongoing undertaking, combined with nature's healing regrowth, has slowly begun to restore the valley's natural ecological processes. In 1980, the national park was designated a World Heritage Site; in 1983, it was named a Biosphere Reserve; and in 1994, the National Park Service and State of California Department of Parks and Recreation signed a Cooperative Management Agreement.

In addition to logging, highway construction has from time to time also posed serious threats to already "saved" redwoods. In the 1960s, there was a close-won victory against proposals that would have slashed four-lane freeways through many dedicated memorial groves in the heart of Prairie Creek Redwoods and part of the 7,000-acre National Tribute Grove in Jedediah Smith Redwoods. In 1995, NPCA joined a coalition of environmental groups, including the Save-the-Redwoods League, urging the California Department of Transportation to reconsider a major highway realignment in the Del Norte Coast Redwoods, which would have involved cutting down more than 200 virgin-growth redwoods. In late 1997, the department issued its decision to make only minimal changes, thereby sparing virtually all of the irreplaceable ancient trees.

OUTSTANDING FEATURES

Among the many outstanding features of the park are the following: **Tall Trees Grove**, where the world's tallest known tree soars to 367 feet; **Gold Bluffs Beach**, a seven-mile stretch of dunes, sandy beach, and bluffs flecked with slivers of gold; **Fern Canyon**, an exquisitely beautiful 50-foot-deep gorge, the sheer walls of which are covered with delicate maidenhair ferns; **Lady Bird Johnson Grove**, offering an excellent interpretive introduction to the park, at the site where the wife of President Lyndon B. Johnson dedicated the park in 1968; and the lower stretch of the **Smith River**, the last major undammed river in California.

PRACTICAL INFORMATION

When to Go

The park is open year-round, and each season offers a pleasant visit; however, crowds are most prevalent in summer. Spring and fall are the seasons for bird migrations and colorful displays of wildflowers and autumn foliage, and temperatures are delightful. Almost the entire annual precipitation occurs from October to April, which may cause flooding along the Klamath River.

How to Get There

By Car: U.S. Route 101, between Eureka and Crescent City, runs north-south through parts of the park; and U.S. Route 199, just east of Crescent City, runs through the north end of the park, in the Jedediah Smith Redwoods.

By Air: Airports in Crescent City and Eureka.

By Train: Amtrak (800-872-7245) stops in Sacramento, where Thruway Bus Connections are provided (see below).

By Bus: Greyhound Lines (800-231-2222) stops in Arcata, McKinleyville, and Eureka, where rental cars are available. Amtrak's Thruway Bus Connections serve Eureka, Arcata, and Crescent City.

Fees and Permits

There are no entrance fees. Free permits are required for backcountry camping and vehicle access to the Tall Trees Grove trailhead. State fishing licenses are required and can be purchased at hardware and tackle shops.

Visitor and Information Centers

Park Headquarters Visitor Center: Open daily all year, 8 a.m.-5 p.m., at 2nd and K streets in Crescent City. Interpretive exhibits, programs, publications, and trail maps.

Hiouchi Information Center: Open daily 9 a.m.-5 p.m., May through October, just off U.S. Route 199 at the Jedediah Smith Redwoods. Interpretive exhibits, summer interpretive programs, publications, and trail maps.

Redwood Information Center: Open daily all year, 9 a.m.-5 p.m., just off U.S. Route 101, on the coast just west of Orick. Interpretive exhibits, summer interpretive programs, publications, and trail maps.

Facilities

Marked trails, wayside exhibits, picnic areas, drinking water, campstore, solar and hot showers, gasoline, sanitary dumps, guided kayak trips, grills, overlooks, and horse rentals.

Handicapped Accessibility

Dolason Prairie, Redwood Information Center, Lost Man Creek, Prairie Creek Visitor Center, Big Tree Wayside, High Bluff, Klamath Overlook, Lagoon Creek, Mill Creek, Crescent Beach Overlook, Crescent Beach, and Hiouchi Information Center are all wheelchair accessible. Accessible campground restrooms are available at Jedediah Smith, Mill Creek, and Prairie Creek. Some trails are accessible, and Revelation Trail is specifically designed for the visually impaired. An excellent access guide is available free from the information centers. TDD is 707-464-6101.

57

▲ *Lost Man Creek, Redwood National Park, California*

Medical Services

First aid is available in the park. Hospitals are in Crescent City and Arcata.

Pets

Pets must remain on leashes not to exceed six feet in length. They are not permitted in the backcountry, on trails, or in public buildings. They are welcome at Crescent and Gold Bluffs beaches, the parking and picnic areas of Redwood Information Center, Lost Man Creek, and the Freshwater Spit overnight use area.

Safety and Regulations

For your safety and enjoyment and for the protection of the park, please follow these regulations and suggestions:

- Because undertows and rip currents are very strong, swimming along the open ocean is not recommended.

- Be alert for loose rocks along cliffs, falling redwood limbs, and poison oak.

- Drive cautiously in fog.

- Follow park regulations regarding bears and food storage (which also pertains to Roosevelt elk and mountain lions).

- Mushroom gathering is prohibited.

- Many roads are narrow, steep, and winding and may not be suitable for large motorhomes or trailers, specifically Howland Hill Road, Lost Man Creek Road, Bald Hills Road, and Coastal Drive between High Bluff and Flint Ridge.

- Fruits and berries may be gathered, but nothing else may be disturbed or removed from the park.

- Remember that it is unlawful to feed, disturb, capture, or hunt wildlife in the national or state parks. A good slogan for helping to protect these parklands is to "leave only footprints."

ACTIVITIES

Hiking, birdwatching, auto tours, canoeing, guided kayak trips, horseback riding, fishing (fresh and saltwater), swimming, whale watching, nature walks and talks, evening campfire programs, picnicking, and camping. Further information is available in the park's newspaper, *Redwood National Park & State Parks Visitor Guide*.

Hiking Trails

Approximately 150 miles of trails wind through the national and state parks, among which are the following: **Lady Bird Johnson Trail**, a one-mile self-guided, interpretive loop trail just off the Bald Hills Road, which provides an excellent introduction to the national park and a magnificent grove of virgin-growth coast redwoods; **Tall Trees Grove**, a 1.3-mile trail from the trailhead, descending steeply 800 feet down to the flats along Redwood Creek to the tallest known tree in the world (a free pass, available at any of the visitor centers, is required to get onto the Tall Trees access road); **Redwood Creek Trail**, an 8.5-mile hike up Redwood Creek Valley to the Tall Trees Grove (camping is allowed only on gravel bars along the creek, but not within a quarter-mile of the Tall Trees Grove; and the National Park Service cautions hikers that there are two crossings of Redwood Creek with bridge crossings provided only during summer because, during periods of heavy winter rains, the creek becomes too dangerous to cross); **Fern Canyon Trail**, at the end of the narrow, unpaved Davison Road, in Prairie Creek park, an easy .7-mile loop path leading from the beach through this delightful little sheer-walled gorge that cuts into the Gold Bluffs where walls are covered with maidenhair ferns; **James Irvine Trail**, running 4.2 miles through the heart of the Prairie Creek groves, following Godwood and Home creeks from Elk Prairie to Fern Canyon and Gold Bluffs Beach; **Elk Prairie Trail**, an easy 2.3-mile trail, often affording opportunities to see Roosevelt elk at Prairie Creek park; **Mill Creek Trail**, a 2.6-mile trail along Mill Creek in Del Norte Coast park; **Frank D. Stout Memorial Grove Trail**, an easy half-mile walk to this magnificent grove and the 340-foot-tall Stout Tree in Jedediah Smith park; **Mill Creek Trail**, a 2.6-mile hike upstream along the beautiful lower stretch of Mill Creek to the Howland Hill Road in Jedediah Smith park; and stretches of the **Coastal Trail** following the ruggedly scenic coast almost continuously from one end of the park to the other.

Scenic Drives

Recommended drives include the following: **Bald Hills Road**, passing the spur to the Lady Bird Johnson Grove and providing views from the ridge along the east side of Redwood Creek Valley; **Newton B. Drury Scenic Parkway**, the ten-mile main road through the Prairie Creek Redwoods, named in honor of the man who for many years, beginning in 1918, headed the Save-the-Redwoods League and was a former director of both the National Park Service and California state parks; **Davison Road**, a nine-mile narrow, unpaved road to Gold Bluffs Beach; and **Howland Hill Road**, a 12-mile narrow, unpaved road winding through a magnificent stretch of lush forest in the Jedediah Smith Redwoods.

OVERNIGHT STAYS

Lodging and Dining

No lodging or dining facilities are available within the park. However, nearby communities such as Crescent City, Klamath, Orick, and Eureka/Arcata offer lodgings and restaurants.

Campgrounds

Campground reservations (made by calling ParkNet at 800-444-7275) are required for the state park campgrounds located within the national park from about mid-May through August. In the rest of the season they are on a first-come, first-served basis. The limit of stay is 15 days from June to September; during the rest of the year it is 30 days. In state park campgrounds, campers with dogs must have proof of rabies vaccinations and pay an additional fee. Trailers up to 27 feet and motorhomes up to 31 feet are allowed at Jedediah Smith and Del Norte Coast campgrounds. Trailers up to 31 feet and motorhomes up to 36 feet are allowed at Prairie Creek campgrounds. RVs longer than 20 feet are not permitted at Prairie Creek Redwoods' campground and Gold Bluffs Beach because the access road is narrow and winding.

Backcountry Camping

Backcountry camping is allowed at campsites on a first-come, first-served basis. The park recommends camping from June through September. Food must be stored in bear-proof containers or hung high from trees to avoid attracting black bears.

FLORA AND FAUNA (Partial Listings)

Mammals: black bear, Roosevelt elk, black-tail (mule) deer, mountain lion, bobcat, coyote, gray fox, marten, mink, sea otter, river otter, longtail and shorttail weasels, beaver, muskrat, mountain beaver, porcupine, raccoon, ringtail, spotted and striped skunks, brush rabbit, grampas, gray and Douglas squirrels, golden-mantled and California ground squirrels, red squirrel (chickaree), red tree vole, Townsend's chipmunk, northern elephant and northern fur seals, California and northern sea lions, harbor and Dall porpoises, Pacific white-sided and Risso (grampus) dolphins, and gray whales.

Birds: Pacific and common loons, western grebe, cormorants, tufted puffin, common murre, pigeon guillemot, rhinoceros and Cassin's auklets, marbled murrelet, wood duck, white-winged, surf, and black scoters, sooty and pink-footed shearwaters, Leach's and fork-tailed storm-petrels, brown pelican, gulls (western, California, Heermann's, and glaucous-winged), great blue heron, black oystercatcher, black turnstone, sanderling, ruffed and blue grouse, California quail, black-shouldered kite, northern harrier, red-tailed hawk, bald eagle, osprey, kestrel, owls (barn, western screech, great horned, northern saw-whet, pygmy, and spotted), belted kingfisher, Anna's and Allen's hummingbirds, woodpeckers (pileated, hairy, and downy), flicker, olive-sided and Pacific-slope flycatchers, western wood pewee, black phoebe, Vaux's swift, crow, raven, scrub and Steller's jays, black-capped and chestnut-backed chickadees, bushtit, red-breasted nuthatch, brown creeper, wrens (house, winter, Bewick's, and marsh), dipper, ruby- and golden-crowned kinglets, robin, thrushes (varied, Swainson's, and hermit), vireos (solitary,

Hutton's, and warbling), warblers (yellow-rumped, Townsend's, hermit, black-throated gray, MacGillivray's, yellow, orange-crowned, yellowthroat, and Wilson's), northern oriole, western tanager, sparrows (white- and golden-crowned, fox, song, and savannah), rufous-sided towhee, dark-eyed junco, black-headed and evening grosbeaks, lazuli bunting, house and purple finches, pine siskin, and American and lesser goldfinches.

Amphibians and Reptiles: Pacific giant, slender, and 13 other species of salamanders, rough-skinned newt, Pacific tree frog, western toad, western fence lizard, and gopher snake.

Trees, Shrubs, and Flowers: coast redwood, knobcone pine, Sitka spruce, western hemlock, Douglas fir, grand (lowland) fir, California laurel (pepperwood), tanoak, Oregon white oak, red alder, black cottonwood, Pacific rhododendron, western azalea, Pacific madrone, Pacific dogwood, bigleaf and vine maples, mountain lilac (blueblossom), red bilberry, California huckleberry, salal, western wahoo, yellow bush lupine, poison oak, skunk cabbage, Douglas's iris, lilies (Bolander's, Columbia, checker, and leopard), firecracker flower, Andrews' clintonia, foxglove, purple lupine, yellow monkeyflower, oxalis, redwood sorrel, western wood anemone, starflower, yellow sand verbena, powdery dudleya, sea rocket, western trillium, western dog and redwood violets, buttercup, calypso orchid, larkspur, wild cucumber, and sword, deer, maidenhair (five-finger), lady, wood, and licorice ferns.

NEARBY POINTS OF INTEREST

The areas surrounding Redwood National Park offer many exciting natural attractions that can be enjoyed as day trips or overnight excursions. Located within and around the park are Prairie Creek Redwoods, Jedediah Smith Redwoods, and Del Norte Coast Redwoods state parks. Directly north of Crescent City is Lake Earl State Wildlife Area; directly east of the park are Six Rivers, Klamath, and Trinity national forests. Along the coast at the south end of the park are Humboldt Lagoons State Park, Harry A. Merlo State Recreation Area, Patricks Point State Park, and Trinidad State Beach. The Samoa Dunes lie just outside Eureka.

SEQUOIA AND KINGS CANYON NATIONAL PARKS

▲ *Fire scars on giant sequoias*

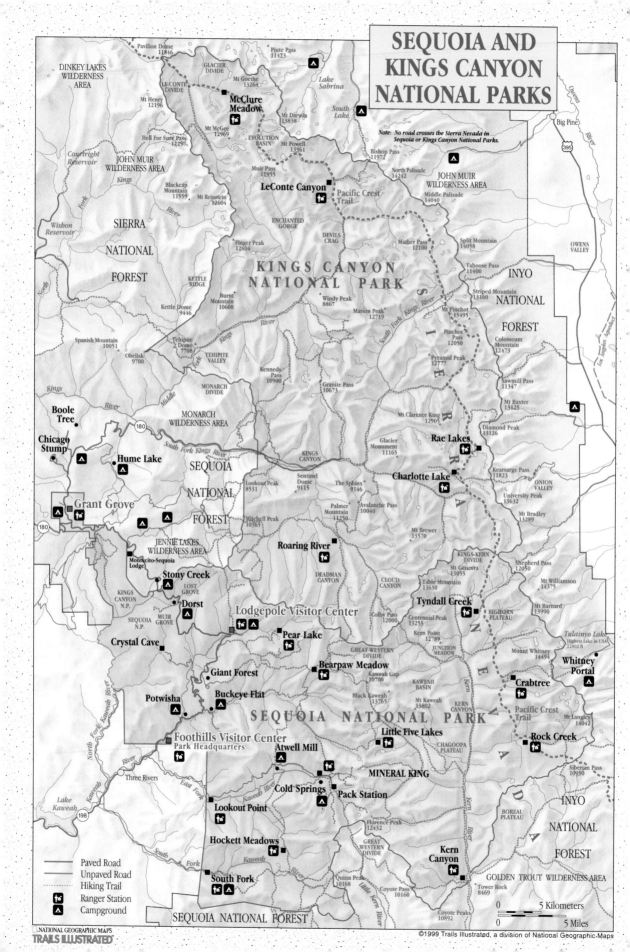

SEQUOIA AND KINGS CANYON NATIONAL PARKS

Note: *No road crosses the Sierra Nevada in Sequoia or Kings Canyon National Parks.*

Legend

——	Paved Road
——	Unpaved Road
····	Hiking Trail
■	Ranger Station
⛺	Campground

0 ___ 5 Kilometers
0 ___ 5 Miles

Sequoia and Kings Canyon National Parks

Three Rivers, CA 93271-9700
559-565-3341

Sequoia and Kings Canyon are adjoining national parks, with a combined area of 864,383 acres. They protect deep mountain canyons and valleys, great mountain peaks, alpine-lake-dotted High Sierra wilderness, an abundance of wildlife, and magnificent groves of the world's largest tree, the massive giant sequoia (*Sequoiadendron giganteum*), in the southern Sierra Nevada of California. Mount Whitney, the highest peak in the 48 contiguous states, rises to 14,495 feet elevation at the eastern edge of Sequoia National Park. From such rugged peaks along the Sierra Crest, elevations in these parks gradually descend down the west slope of the Sierra to foothills chaparral at 1,500 feet. Within this tremendous range of elevations is an ecologically rich diversity of flora and fauna and breathtaking scenery. This is a land that inspired naturalist-author John Muir and countless others to stand in awe of what Muir called this "sublime wilderness."

Sequoia was established as a national park on September 25, 1890; Kings Canyon began as General Grant National Park six days later and was greatly expanded and renamed in 1940. Both parks were named Biosphere Reserves in 1976, and much of both parks was designated wilderness in 1984.

OUTSTANDING FEATURES

In Sequoia:

Among the many outstanding features of this park are the following: **Giant Forest**, with beautiful meadows and the famous giant sequoia grove; **General Sherman Tree**, the largest living thing in the world at 2.8 million pounds and 274 feet tall and estimated to be more than 2,000 years old; **Moro Rock**, a huge granite monolith dome providing a sugar-pine-framed panorama of Kaweah Canyon and the snowy peaks of the Great Western Divide; **Crescent Meadow**, a beautiful, forest-edged meadow between Giant Forest and Moro Rock; marble **Crystal Cave** with its decorative stalactites and stalagmites; **Tharps Log**, the oldest pioneer cabin remaining in the park, built in the 1860s at the end of a giant sequoia log; **Mineral King**, a spectacular glacial valley that was saved from becoming a Disney Corporation resort by a successful Sierra Club lawsuit and added to the park in 1978; **Hospital Rock**, a former homesite of Indians from prehistoric times to the 1870s, with pictographs and grinding holes; and **Pear Lake**, a jewel set amid the beauty of a glaciated, hard-rock basin.

In Kings Canyon:

Among the many outstanding features of this park are the following: **General Grant Tree**, at 267 feet tall and 107 feet in circumference the third largest tree on earth, also known as the "nation's Christmas tree"; **Grant Grove**, a stand of 2,000- to 3,000-year-old trees; **Panoramic Point**, a magnificent view of the High Sierra; magnificent **Big Stump Trail**, featuring the remains of early logging; **Centennial Stump**, a sequoia cut down for exhibition at the 1876 centennial in Philadelphia; **Cedar Grove**, the sheer-walled, U-shaped, mile-deep valley of the South Fork of the Kings River (reached by road, in summer only); **Roaring River Falls** and **Mist Falls**, reached by trails from Cedar Grove; **Reflection Lake**, a magnificent lake in a deep canyon; **Rae Lakes**, a magical cluster of High Sierra lakes along the Pacific Crest Trail; and **Tehipite Valley**, the awesome 3,000-foot-deep, three-mile-long, sheer-walled canyon of the Middle Fork of the Kings River (reached only by wilderness trail).

When this national park was expanded and renamed in 1940, both valleys of Cedar Grove and Tehipite were excluded because they were designated reclamation withdrawals for proposed reservoirs to serve agricultural interests. But with the urging of NPCA and other environmental groups, Congress in 1965 finally eliminated the withdrawals and added these incredible places to the park.

When to Go

The parks are open-year round, but some areas and State Route 180 into Cedar Grove are closed in the winter. October through April is the wet season, providing about 90 percent of the annual precipitation. Temperatures remain mild at lower elevations. Cross-country skiing is popular in winter. Tire chains may be necessary when it is snowing on mountain roads. May through September is generally the hot, dry season, while spring and autumn are usually delightful. Wildflowers bloom over a long period, beginning at the lower elevations as early as January and continuing into October.

How to Get There

By Car: From State Freeway 99 at Visalia, drive east 58 miles on State Route 198 to the Giant Forest; or from State Freeway 99 at Fresno, drive east 54 miles to the Grant Grove part of Kings Canyon National Park. The Generals Highway connects Giant Forest and Grant Grove, making a loop trip possible. The 25-mile road from Grant Grove to Cedar Grove winds through a stretch of Sequoia National Forest before reentering the park. A narrow, unpaved 25-mile spur road up to Mineral King Valley branches southward from Route 198 between Three Rivers and the Ash Mountain park entrance, entering the park in about ten miles.

By Air: Airport in Fresno.

By Train: Amtrak (800-872-7245) stops in Hanford and Fresno.

By Bus: Greyhound Lines (800-231-2222) stops in Visalia. Small tour companies operate from Fresno and Visalia.

Entrances

Kings Canyon entrance: Highway 180 (Kings Canyon Highway) east from Fresno.
Sequoia entrance: On Highway 198 northeast of Three Rivers at Ash Mountain, or northeast of Pinehurst at Grant Grove.

Fees and Permits

Entrance fees are $10 per vehicle and $5 per person on foot, bicycle, or motorcycle. Buses vary according to capacity. Free backcountry permits are required; see "Backcountry Camping" below for important details. State fishing licenses are required and available from local stores.

Visitor and Nature Centers and Ranger Stations

Foothills Visitor Center in Sequoia: Open year-round. Interpretive exhibits, publications, maps, schedules, and permits.

Lodgepole Visitor Center in Sequoia: Open daily year-round. Interpretive exhibits, audiovisual programs, publications, maps, schedules, and permits.

Mineral King Ranger Station in Sequoia: Open in summer. Information and maps.

Nature Center in Sequoia: Open daily July 1 to Labor Day. Interpretive exhibits and hands-on activities.

Cedar Grove Ranger Station in Kings Canyon: Open daily in summer. Information and maps.

Grant Grove Visitor Center in Kings Canyon: Open daily year-round. Interpretive exhibits, publications, maps, schedules, and permits.

The Giant Forest Museum is planned for opening in 2001 or 2002 in the Giant Forest, providing interpretive exhibits and programs on the ecology and history of the Giant Sequoia.

Facilities

Groceries, camping and picnic supplies, lodgings, restaurants, cafeterias, snack bars, gift shops, post offices, hot showers, pack stations and stables for horse rentals, and laundry. Note: There are currently NO SERVICE STATIONS in these parks. Fuel is available in such nearby communities as Three Rivers and at Kings Canyon Lodge and Hume Lake along the road to Cedar Grove.

Handicapped Accessibility

Restrooms in visitor centers and most campgrounds are wheelchair accessible. In these campgrounds, at least one site has an extended table. A detailed chart is available by contacting park headquarters.

Medical Services

First aid is available at visitor centers or from rangers. Hospitals are in Fresno, 50 miles from Kings Canyon (Grant Grove), and in Exeter, 50 miles from Sequoia (Giant Forest).

Pets

Pets must remain on leashes not to exceed six feet in length or be otherwise physically restrained. They are not permitted on any trails or in the backcountry. Kennel services are available in Visalia and Fresno.

Safety and Regulations

For your safety and enjoyment and for the protection of the park, please follow these regulations and suggestions:

- Be extremely cautious in and around rivers and streams as they can be treacherous, with slippery rocks, fast currents, and cold temperatures. Do not swim above waterfalls or in swift water.

- Rattlesnakes are found almost everywhere in the park; watch where you place your hands and feet.

- Check often for ticks.

- When thunderstorms threaten, do not stand under a natural lightning rod, such as an isolated tree, and avoid standing above the surrounding landscape, such as ridges or on Moro Rock.

- Because many park roads are narrow, steep, and winding, the maximum vehicle lengths permitted on the Generals Highway are 40 feet for a single vehicle and 50 feet for a combination vehicle.

- Vehicles and bicycles are not permitted on any park trails.

- Remember that it is unlawful to feed, disturb, capture, or hunt park wildlife or to damage, collect, or cut down trees and other plantlife.

The National Park Service asks visitors not to litter the park with trash. An excellent slogan to remember as a guide to protect these parks is to "leave only footprints."

ACTIVITIES

Hiking, birdwatching, horseback riding and wilderness pack trips, bicycling, mountain climbing, Crystal Cave tours, auto tours, bus tours, interpretive walks and talks, children's programs, interpretive exhibits, cross-country skiing, snowshoeing, sledding, picnicking, camping, fire-management demonstrations, night sky watches, field seminars, and fishing. Further information is available in the park's newspaper, *Sequoia-Kings Canyon National Parks & Sequoia National Forest*.

Horseback and Wilderness Pack Trips

Horseback riding and wilderness pack trips have long been popular in these parks. For information and reservations from day and spot trips up to fully outfitted and guided stock trips into the High Sierra wilderness, contact Grant Grove and Cedar Grove stables at 209-565-3464 and the Wolverton and Mineral King pack stations at 209-565-3039 (in summer) or 520-855-5885 (in winter).

Hiking Trails

There are roughly 700 miles of trails in these parks. Some of the most interesting and exciting are the following:

In Sequoia:
Congress Trail, an easy, two-mile, mostly paved path, beginning near the General Sherman Tree, the world's largest tree, and leading through a magnificent stretch of the Giant Forest sequoias; **Moro Rock Trail**, a 1.7-mile hike starting at the Giant Forest and leading out to this huge granite monolith (plus .3-mile to the summit of the rock), offering a spectacular panorama of the Great Western

Divide's 12,000-foot peaks (the Moro Rock-Crescent Meadow Road, which also leads to the rock, is reached by shuttle service from the Giant Forest); **Sugar Pine Trail**, leading two miles between Moro Rock and Crescent Meadow; **Crescent Meadow Loop Trail**, a mile loop around this exquisite meadow; **Huckleberry Trail**, a three-mile hike between the Giant Forest and Crescent Meadow; **Eagle Lake Trail**, a 3.5-mile hike up to Spring Creek, with the steepest climb on up to Eagle Sink Holes and on to the little lake; **Lakes Trail**, a day-long, six-mile hike from Wolverton up along the top of Tokopah Cliffs to Pear Lake—a jewel set in a beautiful, glaciated, hard-rock basin; and the **Pacific Crest Trail** and **John Muir Trail** (the same route through much of this park), running north-south, the latter ending atop Mount Whitney; and the **High Sierra Trail**, *one of the premier hikes* in the entire National Park System, leading 81 miles from Crescent Meadow, into the spectacular Kern River Canyon, climbing into the most rugged part of the High Sierra, passing by or near dozens of sparkling alpine lakes in glacier-sculpted basins, scaling the summit of Mount Whitney, and then rapidly descending the east face of the Sierra in the Inyo National Forest to Whitney Portal (many visitors enjoy hiking stretches of this trail at various times, while others hike the entire trail from one end to the other).

In Kings Canyon:
General Grant Tree Trail, an easy half-mile loop through this spectacular grove to the General Grant Tree; **Redwood Mountain Trail**, which runs about three miles along the ridge of Redwood Mountain to the Sugar Bowl Grove in the Grant Grove unit of this park; **Redwood Mountain-Redwood Canyon Loop Trail**, a hike of about seven miles that reveals the effects of sequoia fire ecology; **Panoramic Point Trail**, a quarter-mile trail at the end of a steep, narrow spur road providing a grand view of the Sierra Nevada; **River Trail**, an easy half-mile walk at Cedar Grove from the South Fork Kings River to powerfully plunging Roaring River Falls; **Zumwalt Meadow Trail**, an easy one-mile loop at Cedar Grove; the **Trail to Mist Falls**, a day-long hike of five miles from the road's end at Zumwalt Meadow up to this spectacular waterfall in Paradise Valley

and providing awesome views of the glacially widened gorge of the South Fork Kings River; **Rae Lakes Loop**, a four- to five-day hike (partly on the Pacific Crest Trail) through this magical cluster of High Sierra lakes; and **High Sierra Trail, John Muir Trail**, and **Pacific Crest Trail** (following the same route), running north-south through the park.

OVERNIGHT STAYS

Lodging and Dining

In Sequoia:. Options include:

Wuksachi Village, open for the first time in 1999, providing motel-type lodging, with a dining room and gift shop in the main lodge building. For reservations, call Delaware North Parks Services.

Lodgepole, offering a market, deli, and ice cream shop, open from mid-May to mid-October.

Bearpaw Meadow Camp, offering a tent hotel for hikers from mid-June to mid-September. Meals and showers.

In Kings Canyon: Options include:

Grant Grove Village, offering cabins (individual and four-plex units) and motel-type lodgings all year, with a restaurant, gift shop, and market.

Cedar Grove Lodge, open from May through September, offering motel-type rooms, with restaurant and gift shop.

For reservations at both places, call Kings Canyon Park Services Co. at 209-335-5500.

The gateway community of Three Rivers also offers lodgings and restaurants. Especially during the peak of season, please consider using these facilities to decrease visitor impact on the park.

Campgrounds

In Sequoia: All non-group campsites, except those at Lodgepole, are available on a first-come, first-served basis. Reservations, which are required for Lodgepole from mid-May through Labor Day, are made through

National Park Reservation Service at 800-365-CAMP. Trailers are prohibited at Atwell Mill, Buckeye Flat, and Cold Springs because the access roads are narrow and steep. Those with trailers should not use South Fork because of a steep, narrow access road and limited turnaround room in the campground. The maximum length of stay is 14 days between June 14 to September 14; for the rest of the year, maximum stay is 30 days. Campgrounds fill up by at least early afternoon from mid-July to Labor Day. Campsites that can accommodate RVs longer than 30 feet long are very limited. Lodgepole has a 32-foot limit. At all campgrounds, food must be kept in provided storage lockers.

In Kings Canyon: All non-group campsites are available on a first-come, first-served basis. The maximum length of stay is 14 days between June 14 and September 14 and 30 total days for the rest of the year. Campsites that can accommodate RVs more than 30 feet long are very limited. Most campgrounds permit a maximum of one vehicle and six people per site. Group camping requires reservations; write Canyon View Campground, Group Sites, Cedar Grove Ranger Station, Box 948, Kings Canyon National Park, CA 93633 or Sunset Campground, Group Sites, Grant Grove Ranger Station, Box 948, Kings Canyon National Park, CA 93633. Groups must include at least 20 people in Cedar Grove and 12 to 20 people in Grant Grove. Cedar Grove campers must keep food in provided storage lockers. Grant Grove campers must store food in vehicle trunks.

Backcountry Camping

Backcountry camping is allowed throughout most of both parks. The National Park Service recommends camping from June through September. A backcountry permit is required; reservations for a permit can be made beginning March 1 for the upcoming camping season, and they must be made at least 14 days in advance by mail. Some permits are also available at the park on a first-come, first-served basis throughout the summer camping season. Campers must hang food high from trees using the counterbalance method or use approved food storage to avoid attracting

bears. Fires are permitted only in designated fire rings or in campstoves and may be prohibited in times of high fire danger.

FLORA AND FAUNA (Partial Listings)

Mammals: black bear, mountain sheep, mule deer, mountain lion, bobcat, coyote, gray fox, badger, pine marten, fisher, longtail and shorttail weasels, raccoon, ringtail, porcupine, spotted and striped skunks, blacktail and whitetail jackrabbits, pika, brush rabbit, desert cottontail, mountain beaver, gopher, western gray squirrel, Belding and California ground squirrels, golden-mantled and Douglas (chickaree) squirrels, and Merriam and lodgepole chipmunks.

Birds: mallard, blue grouse, California and mountain quail, red-tailed hawk, golden eagle, turkey vulture, kestrel, peregrine falcon, owls (western screech, great horned, and spotted), band-tailed pigeon, hummingbirds (Anna's, calliope, and black-chinned), woodpeckers (pileated, acorn, white-headed, hairy, and Nuttall's), western wood-pewee, white-throated swift, violet-green swallow, raven, scrub and Steller's jays, Clark's nutcracker, mountain chickadee, plain titmouse, bushtit, white- and red-breasted nuthatches, brown creeper, wrens (house, winter, Bewick's, rock, and canyon), wrentit, dipper, ruby- and golden-crowned kinglets, California thrasher, robin, Townsend's solitaire, hermit thrush, mountain bluebird, solitary and warbling vireos, warblers (yellow-rumped, hermit, Nashville, MacGillivray's, yellow, orange-crowned, and Wilson's), western tanager, sparrows (white-crowned, fox, song, and Lincoln's), rufous-sided and California towhees, dark-eyed junco, black-headed grosbeak, lazuli bunting, red crossbill, finches (house, purple, and Cassin's), evening grosbeak, and American and lesser goldfinches.

Amphibians and Reptiles: California newt, Pacific tree frog, western toad, western pond turtle, western fence lizard, western terrestrial garter snake, rubber boa, and western rattlesnake. Sadly, both the mountain yellow-legged and foothill yellow-legged frogs, once abundant in the Sierra Nevada, have been rapidly disappearing; the latter is reportedly gone from the southern Sierra. Scientists so far have no definitive answer for their decline.

Trees, Shrubs, and Flowers: Several thousand species of flora have been identified in these parks, including: giant sequoia (*Sequoiadendron gigantea*), pines (western white, sugar, whitebark, foxtail, lodgepole, ponderosa, and Jeffreys), mountain hemlock, white and red firs, incense cedar, California nutmeg, California sycamore, oaks (blue, California black, California scrub, a shrubby form of Oregon white, interior, and canyon live), white alder, black cottonwood, California redbud, Pacific dogwood, California buckeye, bigleaf maple, California bay laurel, Whipple yucca, several manzanitas, ceanothus, western azalea, California fuschia, fairy lantern, California poppy, coneflower, gilia, 20 to 30 species of lupines, Ithuriel spears, monkeyflower, shootingstar, and snow plant.

The areas surrounding Sequoia and Kings Canyon national parks offer many fascinating natural attractions that can be enjoyed as day trips or overnight excursions. Yosemite National Park lies to the north in the Sierra Nevada. The Sierra, Sequoia, and Inyo national forests surround the parks. One of the most challenging and scenic trails anywhere leads from the "back side" of the Sierra Nevada, up from Whitney Portal, just west of U.S. Route 395, switchbacking up to the rock spires of Mount Whitney's summit. Pinnacles National Monument is about 130 miles to the west. The Bureau of Land Management administers many areas around the park, including Crater Mountain, Fish Slough, San Joaquin River/Squaw Leap trails, Case Mountain, Eureka Dunes, North Fork Kaweah River, and the scenic rock formations of the Alabama Hills in the Owens Valley.

YOSEMITE NATIONAL PARK

▲ El Capitan

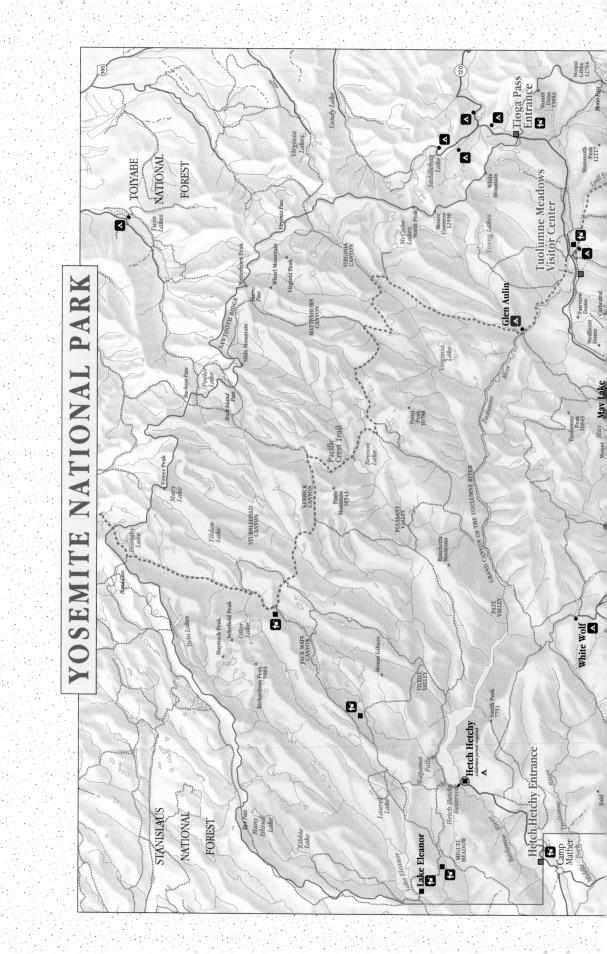

YOSEMITE NATIONAL PARK

INYO

NATIONAL

FOREST

SIERRA

NATIONAL

FOREST

CREST

Koip Peak 12861

Donahue Peak 12861

Donahue Pass

Potter Point

Ireland Lake

Evelyn Lake

Johnson Peak

Vogelsang Peak

CATHEDRAL RANGE

Mount Maclure

Mount Lyell 13114

Mount Florence 13114

Mount Ansel Adams 11760

Foerster Peak 12058

Long Mountain 11502

Isberg Peak

Isberg Pass

Post Peak Pass

Post Peak

Triple Divide Peak

Fernandez Pass

Gale Peak 10693

Sing Peak 10552

Mount Clark 11522

Red Peak 11699

Gray Peak

Merced Peak 11726

CLARK RANGE

Chain Lakes

Chiquito Pass

Merced Pass

Lake

Lake

Vogelsang ▲

Sunrise ▲

Merced Lake ▲ 🏕■

Merced Lake

Little Yosemite Valley ▲

LITTLE YOSEMITE VALLEY

Illilouette Fall

Glacier Point ■

Mount Starr King 9092

MERCED

Buena Vista Peak 9709

BUENA VISTA

Moraine Mountain

Buck Camp 🏕

Ostrander Lake

Crescent Lake

HORSE RIDGE

Porcupine Flat ▲

Yosemite Creek ▲

Valley Visitor Center 🏕▲ ▲

Yosemite Falls ▲

MONO MEADOW

Bridalveil Creek ▲

WESTFALL MEADOWS

Wawona Dome

Wawona Information Center 🏕▲

Mariposa Grove ▲

YOSEMITE VALLEY

El Capitan 7569

RIBBON MEADOW

Valley View ▲

SUMMIT MEADOW

Badger Pass Ski Area ▲

Tamarack Flat ▲

TURNER RIDGE

Wawona ▲

South Entrance

Fish Camp 🏕▲

To Fresno

41

Arch Rock Entrance 🏕▲

Chiniquapin 🏕

Yosemite West

El Portal

140

Big Oak Flat Entrance ▲

Hodgdon Meadow 🏕

Crane Flat ▲

South Fork Tuolumne River

South Fork Merced River

Merced River

140

To Manteca

120

To Merced

Legend:

Paved Road
Unpaved Road
Hiking Trail
🏕 Ranger Station
▲ Campground
▲ Primitive Campsite
High Sierra Camp
(reservations required)

5 Kilometers
5 Miles

0   1   5 Kilometers
0   1   5 Miles

Yosemite National Park

P.O. Box 577
Yosemite, CA 95389-0577
209-372-0200

From dramatic changes in topography and ecology to the four beautifully distinct seasons, from ever-popular Yosemite Valley to the serenity of the High Sierra wilderness, from the smallest alpine wildflower to the Grizzly Giant (the largest of the park's massive sequoias, estimated to be at least 2,700 years old), from the smallest dashing mountain rivulet to the peaceful meanders of the Merced River in Yosemite Valley, and from the tiniest alpine tarn to sparkling Lake Tenaya, the park's largest natural body of water—for all of these reasons and more, Yosemite is a true jewel.

Located in the Sierra Nevada of northern California, Yosemite is an inspiringly magnificent 761,236-acre park containing the incomparable, glacier-sculpted Yosemite Valley, towering granite domes and peaks, dashing streams and rivers, thundering waterfalls, wildflower-filled meadows, groves of centuries-old giant sequoias, lake-dotted High Sierra wilderness, and an abundance of wildlife. Among Yosemite Valley's well-known landmarks are 3,600-foot El Capitan, Half Dome, North Dome, Cathedral Spires, the Three Brothers, and an array of such majestic waterfalls as Bridalveil and Yosemite, the latter plunging nearly 2,500 feet in two great leaps. And there are phenomenal views into the valley from Glacier Point, Taft Point, and Tunnel View.

In the mid-19th century, this magical place captured the heart of naturalist-author John Muir, who convinced the nation that it was vitally important to protect for posterity the rare and irreplaceable qualities of awesome beauty and wildness in this part of the Sierra Nevada. Now known as the father of Yosemite, Muir wrote that "no temple made with hands could compare with Yosemite." In 1864, Yosemite Valley and the Mariposa Big Tree Grove were deeded by the U.S. Government to the State of California for a state park; in 1890, the national park was established; and in 1906, the state returned its lands for addition to the

national park. In 1984, 677,600 acres of the park were designated as wilderness, and Yosemite was listed as a World Heritage Site.

Muir's love of this magnificent park is shared by all who come to experience the wonder of its natural grandeur. Yet the park faces numerous challenges, in part because of its popularity. NPCA has, consequently, worked for many years to encourage plans for the reduction of both traffic congestion and urban development in Yosemite Valley. The enormous flood of January 1997—which did more than $175 million in damage to Yosemite Valley roads, visitor lodgings, staff housing, and power, water, and sewer lines—gave park planners a new opportunity to rethink how best to protect this cherished place, enhance the visitor's quality of experience, and plan wisely for the future.

PRACTICAL INFORMATION

When to Go

The park is open year-round. Holiday and summer weekends attract especially large numbers of visitors, so try to plan overnight stays to begin mid-week, and be sure to reserve lodgings, campsites, or backcountry permits well in advance. Expect some crowds as well in late spring and early fall, which are exceptionally beautiful times to visit. May and June are the best months for viewing the waterfalls and blooming wildflowers and for birdwatching as many species are then filling the park with a concert of songs. September and October typically bring a succession of clear, brilliant days, and the colors of autumn foliage peak in October. Winter activities such as cross-country and downhill skiing are popular from late November to mid-April.

How to Get There

By Car: From State Freeway 99 at Manteca, it is east 88 miles on State Route 120 to the Big Oak Flat (west) entrance; from State Freeway 99 at Merced, it is northeast 75 miles on State Route 140 to the Arch Rock (west) entrance; from State Freeway 99 at Fresno, it is north 64 miles on State Route 41 to the Wawona (south) entrance; and from U.S. Route 395 at Lee Vining, it is ten miles to the Tioga Pass (east) entrance. The park is about a 4.5-hour drive from San Francisco and about a six-hour drive from Los Angeles. Portions of Route 120 and Glacier Point Road are closed in winter. Please also consider alternate modes of transportation to the park, as congestion is a problem.

By Air: Fresno Air Terminal and Merced Airport are both served by frequently scheduled flights. Bus service is provided from the Fresno airport to the park.

By Train: Amtrak (800-872-7245) stops in Merced from Oakland, connecting with a Yosemite Gray Line bus to the park. Stops in Fresno connect with Amtrak Thruway Bus Service.

By Bus: Yosemite Gray Line (800-369-7275) stops in Merced at the Amtrak depot, the Greyhound depot, and the Fresno Air Terminal. VIA Bus Lines (209-369-PARK) stops at the Greyhound depot in Merced.

Fees and Permits

Entrance fees, valid for seven consecutive days, are $20 per vehicle or $10 per person on foot, bicycle, motorcycle, horseback or by bus. Free permits are required for backcountry camping (see "Backcountry Camping" below for details). A $10 administrative fee is charged for permits by mail. State angling licenses with valid stamps are required for fishing. You can obtain them in person at concession facilities in Yosemite Valley, Wawona, or Tuolumne Meadows or, prior to your visit, at most area sporting goods stores.

Visitor, Information, and Nature Centers and Museums

Valley Visitor Center: Open daily 8 a.m.-8 p.m. in summer; shorter hours other months. Interpretive exhibits, programs including an orientation slide show and the multilingual *One Day in Yosemite*, publications, maps, schedule of activities, and other information.

Happy Isles Nature Center: Open daily from late May until early September. Interpretive exhibits, ranger-led programs, and children's activities.

Big Oak Flat Information Station: Open daily 8 a.m.-6 p.m. in summer; shorter hours other months. Information, orientation materials, permits, publications, maps, and schedule of activities.

Wawona Information Station: Open daily 8 a.m.-5 p.m. (closed for lunch). Information, orientation materials, permits, publications, maps, and schedule of activities.

Tuolumne Meadows Visitor Center: Open daily 8 a.m.-7:30 p.m.; closed in winter. Information, orientation, publications, maps, and schedule of activities.

Other visitor facilities include the Indian Cultural Exhibit, Yosemite Museum Gallery, Ansel Adams Gallery (photography), and the Yosemite Theatre.

Facilities and Services

Gift shops, bicycle and binocular rentals, mountaineering school, hot showers, laundry, lost and found, recycling centers, child care, theatrical events, auditoriums, food storage lockers, picnic areas, ski schools, equipment rentals, photo processing.

Groceries are available at the Village Store, Degnan's Delicatessen, Curry Village, Yosemite Lodge, Wawona Store, Crane Flat, Tuolumne Meadows Store, and El Portal Market. Service stations are located in Yosemite Valley and at Crane Flat, Wawona, and El Portal. Repairs are made at the Yosemite Valley Garage. Emergency road service is available; call 209-372-8320.

A 24-hour ATM is located in Yosemite Village, just south of the Village Store. Check cashing service is available near the machine for a fee. Fax service is available at Curry Village, Ahwahnee Hotel, Yosemite Lodge, and Wawona Hotel. Post offices are located in Yosemite Village, Yosemite Lodge, Wawona and, in summer only, at Tuolumne Meadows and Curry Village.

Shuttle Buses

Complimentary shuttle service is provided throughout Yosemite Valley from Wawona to the Mariposa Grove of giant sequoias (in summer), between Tenaya Lake and Tuolumne

Meadows Lodge (in summer), and from valley hotels to the Badger Pass Ski Area (in winter). These shuttle buses serve most trailheads, visitor centers, museums, campgrounds, shops, lodges, and restaurants. For more information on shuttles and all bus services, contact the Yosemite Transportation Desk at 209-372-8441. NPCA urges visitors to help reduce congestion by using the shuttle.

Handicapped Accessibility

Parking lots, three free shuttle buses, several food facilities, post office, medical/dental clinic, visitor centers, the Yosemite Museum Gallery, Indian Cultural Exhibit, some trails, Happy Isles Nature Center, campsites in Lower and Upper Pines, the Ahwahnee, Yosemite Lodge, and portions of Curry Village are wheelchair accessible. Other facilities and activities may be accessible with assistance. TDD is 209-372-4726; a TDD is also available to hotel guests for outgoing calls at Curry Village and the Ahwahnee. Captioned orientation slide programs are shown at the Yosemite Valley Visitor Center, and sign language interpretation is available (generally in summer only). The National Park Service offers a detailed accessibility guide.

Medical Services

The Yosemite Medical Clinic and an independent dental office located in Yosemite Valley provide emergency and full-service outpatient care, limited prescription medicines, wheelchair rentals, laboratory service, EKG, X-rays, and physical therapy. The closest hospitals are in Mariposa, Merced, Fresno, and Bridgeport.

Pets

Pets are permitted but not encouraged. They must remain leashed or otherwise physically restrained at all times. They are not permitted on trails, in streams or lakes, in lodgings, in public buildings, or in the backcountry. Rules require that owners walk them on paved paths only. Pet waste disposal is required. For their own safety, pets should never be left unattended either outdoors or in vehicles. Kennel service is available at the Yosemite Valley stables (209-372-8348).

Climate

Yosemite's climate varies by elevation throughout the park. Higher elevations will generally have greater precipitation and lower temperatures. Sierra summers are warm, with low humidity and day-time highs ranging from the 70s at Tuolumne Meadows to the 90s in Yosemite Valley. Winters are usually relatively mild. From November to March, 70 to 90 percent of the annual precipitation normally occurs. March and November are transitional months, when pleasantly warm and sunny days can suddenly turn stormy. However, both spring and autumn generally bring delightful, bright sunny days and cool nights.

Average daily temperature range in Fahrenheit and average daily precipitation for lower elevation areas are as follows:

	AVERAGE DAILY	
Month	Temperature F	Precipitation
January	26-49°	6.2 inches
February	28-55°	6.1 inches
March	31-59°	5.2 inches
April	35-65°	3.0 inches
May	42-73°	1.3 inches
June	48-82°	0.7 inches
July	54-90°	0.4 inches
August	53-90°	0.3 inches
September	47-84°	0.9 inches
October	39-74°	2.1 inches
November	31-58°	5.4 inches
December	26-48°	5.6 inches

Worship Services

Worship services are held at locations throughout the park and in surrounding communities; a detailed listing is available in the Yosemite Guide. Religions represented include Roman Catholic, Baptist, Church of Christ, Church of Jesus Christ of Latter-day Saints, Interdenominational Christian, Seventh Day Adventist, and Baha'i Faith.

Safety and Regulations

For your safety and enjoyment and for the protection of the park, please follow these regulations and suggestions:

- Boil or treat for bacteria all river, stream, and lake waters before drinking.

- Know what hypothermia is and how to avoid and deal with it.

- Be alert for poison oak, ticks, and rattlesnakes.

- Remember that bears, mountain lions, and all wildlife are wild and possibly dangerous; fully inform yourself and your companions about how to avoid or cope with any encounters.

- Do not feed, pet, hunt, capture, or otherwise disturb wildlife in any way; doing so is against the law.

- Do not bring firearms with you; they are strictly prohibited in the park.

- Be extremely careful when crossing rivers, streams, and waterfalls for they can be treacherous with fast currents, cold water, and slippery surfaces.

- Always give the right-of-way to horses and mules on trails.

- Think twice before leaving valuables unattended.

- Motor vehicles and bicycles are required to remain on established roads.

- Fires are permitted only in existing fire rings or campstoves below 9,600 feet and then only during specific times of the day.

- Wood gathering is not permitted in Yosemite Valley, in sequoia groves, or above 9,600 feet.

- Never smoke while in an area with flammable materials.

- Do not litter the landscape with trash. Remember the excellent slogan "leave only footprints" to help protect this national park.

Please request a free copy of the *Yosemite Guide* for information about the park. Remember that personal property damage or loss, injuries, and even fatalities can result from not knowing about or not remaining alert to possible hazards.

ACTIVITIES

Ranger-led activities include a full array of interpretive walks and talks, children's and evening campfire programs, field seminars, junior and senior ranger programs, photography walks and workshops, free art classes, and stargazing. Other activities abound, such as hiking, bicycling, horseback riding, rock climbing, cross-country and downhill skiing (including classes), snowshoeing, ice skating, slide and video presentations, living history demonstrations and stage rides, Native American cultural demonstrations, theater productions, tours (bus, trail, tram), picnicking, camping, fishing, and special seasonal events.

Tours

Tours include the following:

Valley Floor Tour: A two-hour, open-air tram or enclosed motor-coach tour of the best sightseeing points, with interpretive discussions of the valley's history, geology, and flora and fauna.

Glacier Point: A four-hour tour conducted from June to November, covering Yosemite Valley to Glacier Point for the awesome view, 3,200 feet directly above the valley floor.

Big Trees: A one-hour, open-air tram tour conducted from spring to autumn of the spectacular Mariposa Grove of Big Trees.

Mariposa Grove: A six-hour tour conducted from spring to autumn, covering Yosemite Valley to the Mariposa Grove.

Grand Tour: An eight-hour tour conducted from spring to autumn, covering Yosemite Valley to Mariposa Grove and Glacier Point.

Tour tickets may be purchased at the following tour/information desks: Yosemite Lodge, Ahwahnee Hotel, Curry Village (summer), and adjacent to the Village Store (spring to fall) in Yosemite Village. Reservations are required for

76

▲ Vernal Fall, Yosemite Valley, Yosemite National Park, California

all tours except the Big Trees tram tour and shuttle buses. For more information, call 209-372-1240.

Numerous self-guided tours are also available, including a two-hour moonlight tour and self-guided auto tours. These tours should be followed with the aid of the Yosemite Road Guide or the Yosemite Valley Tour cassette tape, both available for purchase at the Yosemite Valley Visitor Center.

Hiking Trails

Among the many trails are the following:

Bridalveil Fall Trail: An easy, quarter-mile walk that starts at Bridalveil Fall parking area and ends near the base of this spectacular, 620-foot waterfall.

Lower Yosemite Fall Trail: An easy three-quarter-mile walk from the Yosemite Valley Visitor Center to near the base of this thundering, 320-foot waterfall. That viewing place can also be reached on a path that begins across the road just north of the Yosemite Lodge complex, an approach that offers a magnificent pine-framed vista of the upper and lower falls.

Yosemite Falls Trail: A strenuous, 7.2-mile round-trip, six-to-eight-hour hike that starts at Sunnyside Campground and climbs 2,700 feet to a spectacular overlook near the top of 1,430-foot Upper Yosemite Fall—the world's second highest free-plunging waterfall.

Vernal-and-Nevada Falls Trail: A moderate-to-strenuous hike that begins at Happy Isles Bridge. Choose the 1.5-mile round-trip, two-to-four-hour hike to 317-foot Vernal Fall or the 3.4-mile round-trip, six-to-eight-hour hike to 594-foot Nevada Fall. This trail is also the start of the John Muir Trail that climbs northeastward to Tuolumne Meadows; winds south through the wilderness High Sierra, national forest lands, Devils Postpile National Monument, and Kings Canyon and Sequoia national parks; and ends at Whitney Portal at the base of the sheer east side of the Sierra.

Four-Mile Trail to Glacier Point: A strenuous, 9.6-mile round-trip, six-to-eight-hour hike that begins at Four-Mile Trailhead and switchbacks 3,220 feet up to one of the park's most spectacular overlooks. Some visitors pre-

fer riding a bus to Glacier Point and hiking down this trail, which is closed in winter.

Half Dome Trail: A very strenuous, 16.8-mile round-trip, 10-to-12-hour hike that starts at Happy Isles Bridge. This trail passes Vernal and Nevada Falls and climbs along Little Yosemite Valley, before branching from the John Muir Trail and climbing to the 8,842-foot-high summit of Half Dome—4,882 feet directly above the floor of Yosemite Valley. The last 900 feet to the summit is a steep pipe-and-cable climb. This trail is closed in winter.

Pohono Trail: A moderate, 26-mile round-trip, 12-to-16-hour hike that winds along the south rim of Yosemite Valley, between Glacier Point and Tunnel View at Wawona Tunnel.

John Muir and **Pacific Crest Trails** and numerous others lead throughout the High Sierra—through canyons, along dashing streams, over passes, and to such countless magical places as the Cathedral Lakes, Young Lakes, and Smedberg Lake.

About 800 miles of park trails are maintained as well as possible, but during spring, autumn, and winter, they are neither patrolled nor maintained, and hazards may exist. Hikers should ask for a free copy of the *Yosemite Guide* and the handout on hiking, which provide detailed information, safety regulations, and tips to help make your visit both safe and enjoyable.

Fishing

A California state angler's license with a valid stamp is required and must be visibly displayed while fishing. Licenses are available at concession facilities in Yosemite Valley and Wawona all year, and at Tuolumne Meadows and White Wolf during the summer season. A detailed handout on fishing rules and regulations is available from the park.

Horseback Riding

Guided saddle trips and horse rentals are available. Two-hour, half-day, and full-day guided horse and mule trail rides are offered, as well as four- and six-day rides and custom pack trips to the High Sierra camps. For more information, call 209-372-8348. Reservations may be made at tour desks or at the following stables: Yosemite Valley, 209-372-8348; Tuolumne Meadows, 209-372-8427; and Wawona, 209-375-6502.

Lodging and Dining

Reservations for lodging facilities may be made at hotel front desks or in advance by contacting Yosemite Concession Service at 209-252-4848. Summer reservations should be made well in advance for the following facilities:

The Ahwahnee Hotel, a national historic landmark offering spacious rooms, cottages, and parlors all year. Elegant dining room, cocktail lounge, tour desk, concierge, gift shop, tennis courts. Reservations may need to be made up to a year in advance.

Yosemite Lodge, offering deluxe, standard, and European-style rooms and rustic cabins all year. Restaurants, cocktail lounge, tour desk, gift shops.

Curry Village, offering rooms, cabins, and canvas tent cabins from spring to fall and on winter weekends and holidays. Campstore, mountain shop, restaurants, climbing school, ski and bicycle rentals, ice rink.

Housekeeping Tents, developed camping shelters available from spring to autumn. Campstore, laundry, rest rooms, public showers.

Wawona Hotel, a national historic landmark offering rooms from spring to autumn and on winter weekends and holidays. Restaurant, stables, golf course, and tennis courts.

White Wolf Lodge, offering cabins and canvas tent cabins in summer only. Restaurant and campstore.

Tuolumne Meadows Lodge, offering canvas tent cabins in summer only. Restaurant, stables, climbing school, store, service station.

There are many dining facilities in the park with services ranging from snack bars, fast food, cafeterias, and lawn barbecues to casual and elegant dining. Picnic lunches may be ordered at hotel front desks, as well as catering for weddings, group events, family functions, and conferences (call 209-372-1359). Elegant and fine casual dining facilities include:

Four Seasons Restaurant, serving breakfast and dinner at Yosemite Lodge all year;

Mountain Room Broiler, serving dinner at Yosemite Lodge daily from spring to autumn and on winter weekends and holidays;

Ahwahnee Dining Room, serving breakfast, lunch, Sunday brunch, and dinner. Dress code is in effect, and reservations are required (call 209-372-1489). Open all year;

Wawona Hotel Dining Room, serving breakfast, Sunday brunch, lunch buffet, and dinner. Open daily from spring to autumn and on weekends all year. Reservations are advised; call 209-375-6556;

White Wolf Lodge, serving breakfast and dinner. Open in summer only. Reservations advised; call 209-372-8416; and

Tuolumne Meadows Lodge, serving breakfast and dinner. Open in summer only. Reservations required; call 209-372-8413.

Lodging Outside the Park

To decrease the tremendous visitor impact on the park and its facilities especially during peak seasons, NPCA urges visitors to consider patronizing the many facilities outside the park in such communities as Fish Camp, Oakhurst, El Portal, Mariposa, Groveland, and Lee Vining. Contact the Modesto Chamber of Commerce or the California Visitors Bureau for more information.

Campgrounds

Just as Yosemite—"the Incomparable Valley," as it has been called—has inspired countless photographers and painters, it also inspires the many campers who stay within this glacier-carved gorge of sheer granite cliffs and plunging waterfalls. Beyond the valley, camping areas are scattered throughout the park's lake-dotted wilderness high country, at such High Sierra camps as May Lake, Sunrise, Vogelsang, and Merced Lake.

Group camping is available for ten to 30 persons, to a maximum of two campsites. Reservations are required all year for Yosemite Valley and Tuolumne Meadows group campgrounds and for Hodgdon Meadow Campground from April through October; call the National Park Reservation Service at 800-436-PARK. It is strongly advised that reservations be made as early as possible, as sites are in high demand. To make required group camp reservations for Bridalveil Creek and Wawona Group Campgrounds, contact the Wawona District Office, P.O. Box 2027, Wawona Station, Yosemite National Park, CA 95389; 209-372-0563.

Campgrounds that do not require reservations operate on a first-come, first-served basis. Hodgdon Meadows does not require reservations from November through March. The other campgrounds fill up daily in July and August, and it is strongly recommended that campers arrive by no later than early afternoon to obtain a site during the week and before noon on Fridays to secure a site for the weekend.

Following several recommendations can make your visit both safe and enjoyable. Campers must keep a clean campsite and store food in storage boxes provided or out of sight in a vehicle. Never store food or odiferous items in tents. These precautions are essential to avoid attracting black bears, which recognize that containers, coolers, etc. can hold food. In addition, rules prohibit collecting firewood at all times in Yosemite Valley.

Backcountry Camping

Backcountry camping is allowed throughout much of the park all year. A free permit is required and may be obtained in person at Wawona, Yosemite Valley, Big Oak Flat Entrance, or Tuolumne Meadows. At least 50 percent of each trailhead quota is available up to one day in advance on a first-come, first-served basis. Reservations for summer trips may be made year-round by mail for a $3 administrative fee per person. Send dates, specific trailheads where you plan to start and end, your principal destination, number of persons in your group, and number of stock or pack animals, including second-choice dates, to: Wilderness Center, P.O. Box 545, Yosemite,

CA 95389. You may also call 209-372-0740 from 8 a.m. to 5 p.m. daily. Camping parties may include up to 15 people if camping near a trail; off-trail camping parties are limited to eight persons. Campers must keep a clean campsite and hang food high from trees on provided wires or poles or store it in approved bear-proof canisters to avoid attracting black bears. Please practice minimum-impact camping.

FLORA AND FAUNA (Partial Listings)

Mammals: black bear, mule deer, mountain lion, bobcat, coyote, gray fox, marten, fisher, wolverine, river otter, mink, longtail and short-tail weasels, yellow-bellied marmot, ringtail, raccoon, porcupine, pika, mountain beaver, squirrels (Douglas, western gray, Belding, California, and golden-mantled ground), chickaree, and chipmunks (Merriam, Townsend, alpine, lodgepole, long-eared, and yellow pine).

Birds: mallard, spotted sandpiper, blue grouse, mountain quail, peregrine falcon, owls (great gray, great horned, spotted, flammulated, and northern pygmy), belted kingfisher, band-tailed pigeon, calliope hummingbird, woodpeckers (pileated, acorn, white-headed, downy, hairy, and Nuttall's), flicker, Williamson's sapsucker, western kingbird, western wood-pewee, flycatchers (olive-sided, Hammond's, and dusky), black phoebe, white-throated swift, swallows (northern rough-winged, violet-green, and cliff), raven, scrub and Steller's jays, Clark's nutcracker, mountain chickadee, plain titmouse, bushtit, nuthatches (white-breasted, red-breasted, and pygmy), brown creeper, wrens (house, winter, Bewick's, rock, and canyon), wrentit, dipper, ruby- and golden-crowned kinglets, robin, Townsend's solitaire, hermit thrush, vireos (solitary, Hutton's, and warbling), warblers (yellow-rumped, hermit, black-throated gray, Nashville, MacGillivray's, yellow, orange-crowned, and Wilson's), Brewer's and red-winged blackbirds, northern oriole, western tanager, sparrows (white-crowned, chipping, fox, and song), towhees (California, rufous-sided, and green-tailed), dark-eyed junco, grosbeaks (pine, black-headed, and evening), finches (rosy, purple, and Cassin's), red cross-bill, and pine siskin. More than 230 bird species have been recorded in the park. During May, Yosemite Valley becomes an especially magical place when the waterfalls are full, deciduous trees are leafing out, dogwood trees are in bloom, and the valley is filled with the songs of such birds as western tanagers, black-headed grosbeaks, robins, northern orioles, purple finches, winter wrens, and various flycatchers, vireos, and warblers.

Amphibians and Reptiles: California newt, Pacific tree frog, western toad, western fence lizard, western terrestrial garter snake, and western rattlesnake.

Trees, Shrubs, Wildflowers, and Ferns: pines (western white, sugar, whitebark, limber, lodgepole, ponderosa, Jeffrey, digger gray, and knobcone), mountain hemlock, white and red firs, giant sequoia, incense cedar, western juniper, California black oak, interior and canyon live oaks, quaking aspen, black cottonwood, Pacific madrone, California redbud, Pacific dogwood, California buckeye, bigleaf and western mountain maples, mountain mahogany, chamise, ceonothus, manzanita, western azalea, alpine laurel, tiger lilies (camas, Mariposa, Columbia, and Sierra), iris, cow parsnip, foxglove, lupines, monkeyflowers, penstemon, Indian paintbrush, baby blue eyes, goldfields, California poppy, pussy paws, fireweed, monkshood, mule ears, shooting star, mountain violet, stonecrop, owlclover, Sierra primrose, skypilot, goldenrod, bistort, snow plant, and numerous ferns including bracken.

NEARBY POINTS OF INTEREST

The areas surrounding Yosemite National Park offer many exciting natural attractions that can be enjoyed as day trips or overnight excursions. The Stanislaus, Sierra, Inyo, and Toiyabe national forests border the park and connect with Sequoia and Kings Canyon National Parks, to the southeast. Devils Postpile National Monument is about 40 miles away from the park's east entrance. The Bureau of Land Management administers parts of the Merced and Tuolumne rivers, as well as Bodie Bowl and Conway Summit, Crater Mountain, and Fish Slough, all located near the park.

OTHER NATIONAL PARK UNITS IN THE PACIFIC REGION

▲ *Golden Gate Bridge, Golden Gate National Recreation Area, California*

Other National Park Units in the Pacific Region

National Park of American Samoa

Pago Pago, AS 96799-0001
011-684-633-7082

This 9,000-acre national park in the U.S. Territory of American Samoa in the South Pacific protects three scenically outstanding areas. Two areas—one each on Tutuila and Ta'u islands—range from wild coast, lowland forest, and lush tropical rainforest up to cloud forest and sheer volcanic mountains. A third area, on Ofu Island, features a magnificent beach and an ecologically significant coral reef that contains 150 species of coral. Along with tortoise and Pacific boa, terrestrial wildlife includes two species of fruit bats, known as flying foxes (one of which has a three-foot wingspread) and an array of birds, including long-tailed tropicbird, Samoan duck, Samoan pigeon, fruit dove, Samoan owl, and Samoan honeycreeper. One of the park's purposes is to preserve the Samoan people's ancient Polynesian traditions, and archaeological and mythological heritage. Villagers are thus allowed to continue their long-time practice of gathering rainforest plants for medicinal and cultural purposes. Transportation to the islands is by airline flights from Hawaii to Pago Pago on Tutuila, and lodging is available outside the park on all three islands.

Cabrillo National Monument

P.O. Box 6670
San Diego, CA 92106-0670
619-557-5450

Point Loma, at the mouth of San Diego Harbor in southern California, is the location of this 137-acre national monument named for Portuguese navigator Juan Rodriguez Cabrillo who in 1542 sailed up the Pacific coast from Navidad, Mexico, to San Francisco Bay for the King of Spain. From the heights of the point, visitors can watch the annual gray whale migrations from late December through February, explore rich and fascinating tide pools, tour the historic Old Point Loma Lighthouse, and enjoy beautiful views of San Diego Harbor and the Pacific Ocean. Guided and self-guided interpretive walks are available, and the visitor center offers interpretive exhibits, programs, and publications. From the I-5/I-8 freeway, drivers should take the Rosecrans Street junction and turn right onto Canon Street and left onto Catalina to the monument entrance.

California National Historic Trail

Long Distance Trails Office
National Park Service
P.O. Box 45155
Salt Lake City, UT 84145-0155
801-539-4094

This more than 5,600-mile trail includes mid-19th-century overland routes that in the 1840s and 1850s were used by people seeking their fortunes in gold or a new life in California. The routes begin at several locations along the Missouri River, including St. Joseph and Independence, Missouri, and Council Bluffs, Iowa, and end at a variety of sites in California and Oregon. The national historic trail is currently in the planning stage by the National Park Service and cooperating organizations. Three of the many historic highlights along the route are Scotts Bluff National Monument in Nebraska, Fort Laramie National Historic Site in Wyoming, and City of Rocks National Reserve in Idaho.

Channel Islands National Park

1901 Spinnaker Drive
Ventura, CA 93001-4354
805-658-5700

This 249,353-acre national park off the southern California coast near Santa Barbara protects five of the eight Channel Islands and extends to one nautical mile of the submerged land and kelp forests surrounding each island.

▲ Channel Islands National Park, California

These five—Anacapa (which consists of three small islands lying end to end), Santa Cruz, Santa Rosa, San Miguel, and Santa Barbara islands—feature outstanding natural and cultural resources, including marine life ranging in size from microscopic plankton to the world's largest creature, the blue whale. Among the numerous species of seals and sea lions are harbor and elephant seals, northern fur seals, and Steller and California sea lions; in fact, five species of sea lions breed on San Miguel alone. Terrestrial mammals include the spotted skunk and island fox, a small variety of gray fox. Birds include three kinds of storm petrels, pigeon guillemot, Xantus' murrelet, and Cassin's auklet; perhaps most notable is the pelican, which congregates at a rookery on West Anacapa Island, the main breeding ground for this species in the western United States. The park also contains more than 85 rare and endangered varieties of plants.

NPCA and other groups are working to counter threats to this rich and diverse environment. Recently, NPCA won a court settlement that will phase out hunting and grazing operation. Another threat facing the park is the overfishing of commercially important fisheries—notably of abalone—in the waters surrounding the Channel Islands. NPCA, describing this as "a desperate situation," continues to advocate a ban on commercial fishing in park waters and the surrounding national marine sanctuary. NPCA is also currently working with the National Park Service to protect the native flora and fauna of Santa Rosa, the second largest of the park's islands. The Nature Conservancy owns and manages 55,000 acres of 60,000-acre Santa Cruz, the park's largest island.

The main visitor center, which is in Ventura, provides interpretive exhibits, programs, and publications. Other visitor centers are located on East Anacapa and Santa Barbara islands; and a ranger station is located on San Miguel, where a beautiful crescent beach, wind-swept sand dunes, and remnants of a calcified-fossil forest mark the spot where navigator Juan Rodriguez Cabrillo landed in 1542. Island Packers boats take people from the visitor center in Ventura out to the park. For information on day boat trips to Anacapa, Santa Rosa, San Miguel, Santa Barbara, and the east end of Santa Cruz and for overnight visits to the historic Scorpion Ranch on Santa Cruz, call 805-642-7688; to make reservations, call 805-642-1393. Interpretive guided walks and evening programs are offered on East Anacapa, and interpretive walks are available by request on San Miguel, Santa Rosa, and Santa Barbara.

There are campgrounds on East Anacapa, San Miguel, Santa Rosa, and Santa Barbara, as well as a picnic area on East Anacapa (for camping reservations, call National Park Reservation Service at 800-365-CAMP). Park permits are required to camp overnight on the islands and to land boats on San Miguel and Santa Rosa islands. For trips to the west end of Santa Cruz, contact The Nature Conservancy's Santa Cruz Island Project office at 805-962-9111; for permits to land private boats there, call 805-964-7839. To reach the visitor center in Ventura, from northbound U.S. Route 101, exit at Victoria Ave.; from southbound U.S. Route 101, exit at Seaward Ave. Then, follow park signs to Ventura Harbor and the visitor center.

Devils Postpile National Monument

c/o Sequoia-Kings Canyon National Parks
Three Rivers, CA 93271-9700
760-934-2289
(summer); 209-565-3341

One of the world's most spectacular examples of columnar-jointed basalt is found near the dashing waters of the Middle Fork of the San Joaquin River, at 7,600-feet elevation on the west slope of California's Sierra Nevada. Formed when a molten-hot lava flow cooled and cracked around 90,000 years ago, Devils Postpile is a wall of 40- to 60-foot, angular basaltic columns resembling a giant, pine-framed pipe organ. In the southern end of the monument, 101-foot-high Rainbow Falls plunges magnificently down a lava cliff. Among the monument's trees are mountain hemlock, red fir, black cottonwood, quaking aspen, and western white, lodgepole, and Jeffrey pines. The park also features the black bear and birds such as Steller's jay, mountain chickadee, dipper, hermit thrush, Wilson's warbler, western tanager, and red crossbill.

The John Muir Trail (here part of the Pacific Crest Trail) winds north-south through the 798-acre national monument, and King Creek Trail runs southwest-northeast. Trails to the Devils Postpile start at the ranger station and from the Reds Meadow area. Hikers can reach Rainbow Falls on a trail that continues on south from the Devils Postpile, winding mostly through Inyo National Forest, and from a trailhead a short distance south of Reds Meadow.

The monument is open from mid-June through October, during which time guided interpretive walks and evening campfire programs are provided. From late June through early September, day visitors to the monument and the adjacent Reds Meadow area are required to ride the shuttle from Mammoth Mountain Inn. Near the ranger station, a small campground is available from around July 1 to October 15. Other campgrounds are located along the Middle Fork of the San Joaquin River and at Reds Meadow in the national forest. Lodging, dining, camping supplies, fuel, and horses are available at Reds Meadow and Mammoth Lakes. Access to the monument is from the east side of the Sierra Nevada. From U.S. Route 395, drive west ten miles on State Route 203, through Mammoth Lakes, to 9,175-foot Mineret Summit; then drive southward seven miles on a narrow paved road.

Eugene O'Neill National Historic Site

P.O. Box 280
Danville, CA 94526-0280
925-838-0249

Eugene O'Neill (1888-1953) was one of America's most distinguished playwrights, authoring such works as *The Iceman Cometh*, *Long Day's Journey Into Night*, and *Moon for the Misbegotten*. This 13-acre site in Danville, California, about 35 miles east of San Francisco, protects Tao House, where the Nobel Prize winner and four-time Pulitzer Prize winner wrote many plays and where he and his wife Carlotta lived from 1937 to 1944. Self-guided and ranger-guided interpretive tours are available, the latter on Wednesdays through Sundays with reservations. Access to the site from I-680 is at the Diablo Road exit and proceeding to a parking area for the shuttle service to the site.

▲ Rainbow Falls, Devils Postpile National Monument, California

85

Fort Point National Historic Site

P.O. Box 29333
Presidio of San Francisco, CA 94129-
0333
415-556-1693

Fort Point, strategically located at the entrance to San Francisco Bay in northern California, is a classic brick-and-granite coastal defense fortification built in the mid-19th century. The fort was occupied by a U.S. artillery regiment during the Civil War, but shots were never fired from it. Since the erection of the Golden Gate Bridge in the 1930s, the 29 acres of Fort Point have been partly beneath that great span and adjacent to Golden Gate National Recreation Area.

An audiovisual program, publications, and guided tours are available at the visitor center, along with such interpretive exhibits as "Women in U.S. Military History," "The African-American Soldier Experience," and photographs of the Golden Gate Bridge construction. Picnic facilities and ranger-led natural history walks on the adjacent coastal bluffs are also provided. The site is open Wednesdays through Sundays and is closed on Thanksgiving, Christmas Day, and New Year's Day. Access to the site from U.S. Route 101 northbound is at the last exit before the Golden Gate Bridge toll plaza; turn left onto Lincoln Avenue and left again onto Long Avenue and proceed to the site. From U.S. 101 southbound, exit just after the toll plaza, turn left onto Lincoln and left again onto Long and proceed to the site.

Golden Gate National Recreation Area

Fort Mason, Building 201
San Francisco, CA 94123-1308
415-556-0560

This national recreation area encompasses 74,441 acres in San Francisco, San Mateo, and Marin counties in northern California and protects a tremendous variety of spectacular natural scenery, wildlife habitat, historic features, and urban sites. Following the shoreline, this vast parkland contains Pacific Ocean beaches, coves, rocky headlands, wildflower-filled grassy hillsides, ecologically rich valleys, lagoons, marshes, wildlife, historic ships, forti-

fications, and buildings of historic and cultural significance. Activities include hiking, bicycling, birdwatching, guided horseback riding, picnicking, camping, sunbathing, hang-gliding (at Fort Funston), fishing, and boat trips to the former federal prison on Alcatraz Island (call 415-705-1045 for information). Swimming is also available but only rarely advised, and swimmers are urged to be extremely cautious of the hazards of the ocean's surf and undertow. Many scenically exciting trails loop around the grassy Marin Headlands, starting at such places as Rodeo Beach and the end of the Tennessee Valley Road. Adjacent to the Marin County parts of the recreation area, with interconnecting roads and trails, are such other parklands as Mount Tamalpais State Park, Point Reyes National Seashore, and Muir Woods National Monument.

The Presidio, a former U.S. military base, which was recently added to the national recreation area, has been the subject of intense debate over how it can best be managed. NPCA has been a strong advocate of legislation to establish a public trust to manage the Presidio's many historic buildings. Visit the William P. Mott, Jr., visitor center in the main post of the Presidio on Montgomery Street near Lincoln Avenue. Open daily except on Christmas and New Year's Day. For information call 415-561-4323.

Headquarters and the main information center for the site are located at Fort Mason, just north of Bay and Franklin streets. Other information centers are located at the Cliff House, near the north end of Ocean Beach in San Francisco, and at Fort Cronkhite, near Rodeo Beach in Marin County. Most park sites in San Francisco can be conveniently reached by the city's Municipal Railway (MUNI) bus or metro lines (call 415-673-MUNI). The Marin County parts of the recreation area may be reached from U.S. Route 101 at several exits, including just north of the Golden Gate Bridge, leading to the Fort Cronkhite and Rodeo Beach area, and at the Shoreline Drive (State Route 1) exit that leads to the Tennessee Valley, Muir Beach, and Stinson Beach areas. A number of places in or near the Marin County parts of the recreation area are also served from San Francisco by MUNI and Golden Gate Transit (call 415-923-2000).

John Muir National Historic Site

**4202 Alhambra Avenue
Martinez, CA 94553-3883
925-228-8860**

This 344-acre site in Martinez, California, protects the residence of pioneering environmental-protection advocate and author John Muir, who lived here from 1890 until his death in 1914. Mount Wanda, where he and his daughters often enjoyed walking the oak-dotted hillsides of the Alhambra Valley, is also within the site. Founder and first president of the San Francisco-based Sierra Club, Muir championed the virtue of wildness and wilderness, advocated saving magnificent areas of unspoiled natural beauty, influenced President Theodore Roosevelt and the public to value nature for more than its economic potential, and successfully urged establishment of Yosemite National Park. His efforts failed, however, to block construction of a dam in the park, the reservoir of which inundated Hetch Hetchy Valley.

The site provides exhibits and an audiovisual program on Muir's life, writings, philosophy, and accomplishments. A picnic area and both self-guided and guided tours are available, the latter on Wednesdays through Sundays. The site is closed on Thanksgiving, Christmas Day, and New Year's Day. Access is at the foot of the Alhambra Avenue exit, to the north of Route 4.

Juan Bautista de Anza National Historic Trail

**National Park Service
600 Harrison Street, Suite 600
San Francisco, CA 94123
415-744-3975**

This trail traces the route of a six-month Spanish expedition by 30 families and a dozen soldiers under the leadership of Col. Juan Bautista de Anza, who in 1776 sought to establish an overland route from central Mexico to the Golden Gate in California. This national historic trail extends 1,200 miles from Tubac, Arizona, through the desert of southwestern Arizona and southeastern California along the coast to San Francisco. Most of the trail is currently in the planning stage. Several short segments are open to the public, including a 4.5-mile stretch connecting Tumacacori National Historical Park and Tubac Presidio State Historical Park in Arizona.

Lava Beds National Monument

**P.O. Box 867
Tulelake, CA 96134-0867
530-667-2282**

This 46,559-acre area has geological, historical, and ecological significance. The rugged landscape of cinder cones, shield volcanoes, spatter cones, chimneys, and nearly 200 lava-tube caves was formed when volcanic activity spewed forth molten rock and lava. Geologists believe the most recent vulcanism here occurred around 1,100 years ago. This area then provided a natural fortress for the Modoc Indians as they battled the U.S. Army for rights to their native lands in 1872-73. Among the monument's vegetation are ponderosa pine, sagebrush, rabbitbrush, mountain mahogany, fernbush, penstemon, and Indian paintbrush. Wildlife includes mule deer, coyote, bobcat, badger, jackrabbit, ground squirrel, chipmunk, California and mountain quail, golden eagle, short-eared owl, Steller's and scrub jays, Townsend's solitaire, and western bluebirds. Many species of waterfowl also inhabit or migrate through the adjacent Tule Lake National Wildlife Refuge.

A campground and picnic area are available at the monument, and interpretive exhibits, programs, and publications are offered at the visitor center every day except Thanksgiving, Christmas Day, and New Year's Day. In the summer, interpretive walks, cave tours, and evening campfire programs are also provided. Visitors are cautioned to be extremely careful when exploring caves; the National Park Service advises explorers to wear protective headgear, take more than one light source, wear clothing adequate for cool temperatures, and be alert for low cave ceilings, uneven footing, and steep trails. Visitors should also be alert for rattlesnakes. Access to the monument's visitor center is 25 miles south from Tulelake, California.

Manzanar National Historic Site

**c/o Death Valley National Park
P.O. Box 579
Death Valley, CA 92328-0579
619-786-2331**

In the windswept desert of the Owens Valley in eastern California are the remains of the Manzanar Relocation Center, where the U.S. government held captive more than 10,000 Japanese-American men, women, and children during World War II. Gripped by anti-Japanese hysteria during that period, the government took the extraordinary step of holding in ten such detention camps 110,000 Japanese-Americans, 70 percent of whom were American citizens. Only in the 1990s did the government apologize for these actions and pay reparations to those detained.

Manzanar consisted of 576 single-story barracks, in which an entire family lived in a single room measuring 20 by 24 feet. Three historic structures remain: a large building that served as an auditorium and gymnasium, a sentry post, and a police office. Also protected at this 800-acre site are Native American campsites and the remains of an early 20th-century agricultural community. Access to the area is just off U.S. Route 395, ten miles north of Lone Pine or five miles south of Independence.

Muir Woods National Monument

**Mill Valley, CA 94941-2696
415-388-2595**

The coast redwoods (*Sequoia sempervirens*) preserved in this 553-acre national monument are one of the San Francisco Bay area's last uncut stands of old-growth redwoods. The majestic redwood is known for ranging along the coast of California, from the southern end of Monterey County north to near Oregon, and many groves and areas of forest are protected in state parks and Redwood National Park. However, the narrow valley containing these towering trees had been targeted for logging and inundation by a reservoir until this beautiful area was purchased by Congressman William Kent and his wife and donated by them to the federal government in the early 1900s. In 1908, it was established as a national monument honoring conservationist John Muir.

Other trees and plants of ecologically rich Muir Woods are Douglas fir, tan oak, California buckeye, bay, bigleaf maple, red alder, madrone, azalea, oxalis, clintonia, salal, sword fern, lady fern, and bracken. Mule deer, bobcat, gray fox, raccoon, red and gray squirrels, spotted owl, Anna's and Allen's hummingbirds, Steller's and scrub jays, chestnut-backed chickadee, nuthatches, brown creeper, winter wren, and varied thrush are among the many species of wildlife inhabiting the area. Redwood Creek provides winter habitat for steelhead trout and silver salmon.

Trails wind along the creek, switchback up the valley's wooded slopes, and connect with trails in adjacent Mount Tamalpais State Park and nearby Golden Gate National Recreation Area. The monument's visitor center provides interpretive exhibits and publications. Near the center, a concessionaire offers lunch snacks. No picnicking, dogs, bicycling, or motorized vehicles are permitted. Access to the monument is six miles from U.S. Route 101 on State Route 1, but parking is limited. Gray Line Tours provide daily service from San Francisco.

Pacific Crest National Scenic Trail

**U.S. Forest Service
P.O. Box 3623
Portland, OR 97208
503-326-3644**

This national scenic trail extends 2,638 miles from Canada to Mexico. It runs through North Cascades National Park and Lake Chelan National Recreation Area in Washington to Crater Lake National Park in Oregon. In California, the trail crosses Lassen Volcanic and Yosemite national parks, Devils Postpile National Monument, and Sequoia-Kings Canyon national parks.

Pinnacles National Monument

**5000 Highway 146
Paicines, CA 95043-9710
408-389-4485**

This 16,265-acre national monument protects an array of spectacular rhyolite pinnacles, domes, and crags, rising 500 to 1,200 feet, along with caves, volcanic features amid steeply sloping hills in the Gabilan Range of west-central

California. This beautiful, ecologically rich landscape is part of the eroded evidence of ancient volcanic eruptions of at least 23 million years ago. The monument's flora ranges from riparian and valley-bottom species, such as California sycamore, cottonwood, willow, coast live and valley oaks, California buckeye, and blue elderberry, up to slopes covered with dense growths of shrubby chaparral that include red-stemmed and great-berried manzanitas, buckbrush, ceanothus (fragrant when in bloom), toyon, and chamise. The pale, almost smoky-appearing, gray-green Digger pine grows on some chaparral-covered hillsides—in a few places in association with blue oak. Among the spring wildflowers are California poppy, goldfields, lupine, penstemon, larkspur, Indian paintbrush, and shootingstar.

Wildlife of the monument include mule deer, mountain lion, bobcat, coyote, gray fox, raccoon, jackrabbit, gray squirrel, chipmunk, big-eared kangaroo rat, several kinds of bats, kingsnake, northern Pacific rattlesnake, and whiptail and California legless lizards. Birds range from California quail, red-tailed hawk, golden eagle, turkey vulture, and peregrine falcon to Anna's hummingbird, acorn woodpecker, scrub jay, rock wren, wrentit (the most characteristic bird of the chaparral habitat), California thrasher, California (brown) towhee, black-headed grosbeak, white-throated swift, and violet-green swallow.

One of the most scenic hikes is the five-mile round-trip High Peaks Trail that climbs among the heart of the pinnacles. Chalone Creek Trail is a round-trip hike of just under nine miles to the 3,305-foot North Chalone Peak. One-mile, round-trip, self-guided interpretive Caves-Moses Spring Trail winds beneath huge boulders that are lodged in part of Bear Gulch. The National Park Service cautions that only skilled rock climbers and those with professional leaders should engage in rock climbing. Hikers should be alert for rattlesnakes and poison oak.

The visitor center, providing interpretive exhibits, programs, and publications, is on the east side of the monument. A private campground is located just outside the monument's east entrance; for information, call 408-389-4462. A ranger station and campground are on the west side of the monument. Access to the east entrance is 31 miles south of Hollister on State Route 25 and just over two miles west on the spur road; to the west entrance, it is ten miles from U.S. Route 101 at Solidad on State Route 146. Visitors to the west district who are driving large motor homes or pulling trailers are advised to be extremely careful on this narrow, steep, and winding spur road.

Point Reyes National Seashore

Point Reyes, CA 94956-9799
415-663-1092

This 71,057-acre national seashore protects a scenically and ecologically rich part of the northern California coast about an hour's drive north of San Francisco. The area features many miles of Pacific Ocean beaches, sheer cliffs and rocky headlands, tidal lagoons and esteros, lush valleys and forested Inverness Ridge, and expanses of coastal shrub and former dairy farm grasslands. The area is also of great geological interest, since Point Reyes Peninsula is like an "island in time," separated from the mainland mass of California by the San Andreas Fault that runs along Olema Valley and Tomales Bay. Not only are the rock types of the peninsula thus different from those on the east side of the fault zone, but the peninsula itself is attached to a different earth-surface plate, scraping along the western edge of the North American land mass, annually moving about three inches northwestward. Point Reyes also reveals something of the history of the Coast Miwok Indians, English and Spanish explorers, the Mexican "lords of Point Reyes," and 20th-century dairy farmers.

This national seashore's tremendous diversity of flora includes such species as Bishop pine, Douglas fir, California bay, California buckeye, California wax-myrtle, coast and canyon live oaks, bigleaf maple, huckleberry, coffeeberry, salal, manzanita, toyon, ceonothus, coyotebush, California sagebrush, poison oak, coastal bush lupine, sticky and other monkeyflowers, California poppy, buttercup, mission bells, California tiger lily, giant trillium, Douglas iris, orchids, violets, shootingstar, gentian, blue coast gilia, baby blue-eyes, phacelias, forget-me-not, Indian paintbrush, owl's clover, beach primrose, beach aster, seaside daisy, goldfields, sunflowers, and numerous varieties of ferns including sword, deer, and polypody. More than 60 species of plants found on the peninsula are not found east of the fault line.

Mammals include Tule elk, blacktail (mule) deer, mountain lion, bobcat, gray fox, raccoon, porcupine, gray squirrel, and Sonoma chipmunk. Among the more than 450 species of birds are loons, grebes, cormorants, common murre, pigeon guillemot, Cassin's auklet, wood duck, cinnamon teal, surf and white-winged scoters, greater scaup, sooty shearwater, brown pelican, gulls, great blue heron, great egret, black-bellied and snowy plovers, marbled godwit, long-billed curlew, willet, sanderling, black turnstone, California quail, black-shouldered kite, northern harrier, osprey, band-tailed pigeon, Anna's and Allen's hummingbirds, acorn woodpecker, swallows (violet-green, cliff, and barn), scrub and Steller's jays, chestnut-backed chickadee, bushtit, pygmy nuthatch, winter and marsh wrens, wrentit, varied and hermit thrushes, warblers (yellow-rumped, Townsend's, yellow, orange-crowned, yellowthroat, and Wilson's), red-winged blackbird, meadowlark, sparrows (white-crowned, golden-crowned, fox, song, and savannah), rufous-sided and California (brown) towhees, black-headed grosbeak, and purple finch.

The list of visitor activities begins with birdwatching, for Point Reyes is obviously a birder's mecca. Camping is available at four walk-in campsites; the required permits are available at the visitor center. Wading is also popular at Drake's and Limantour beaches and even, with great caution, at McClures and Kehoe beaches where heavy surf and dangerous currents often prevail. At Great Beach, however, pounding surf, rip tides, and undertow are extremely hazardous and prevent swimming altogether. Also available are hiking, picnicking, bicycling, and horseback riding (though restrictions apply to trail use).

Of the more than 140 miles of trails looping through the national seashore, one of the major trailheads is adjacent to Bear Valley Visitor Center, where interpretive exhibits, programs, and publications are provided. One of the most delightful trails winds four miles through forested Bear Valley to the coast at Arch Rock. Other trails lead from the end of Limantour Road; from the visitor center at Drake's Beach; from the end of the Mount Vision Road; to the 1,407-foot-high summit of

Mount Wittenberg, highest point on Point Reyes Peninsula; and from the end of Pierce Point Road in the Tule Elk Refuge at the north end of the peninsula.

Except for light snacks provided by a concessionaire next to the Drakes Beach visitor center, meals and lodging are available only in nearby towns and cities. Other parklands adjacent to or near Point Reyes are Golden Gate National Recreation Area and Tomales Bay and Samuel P. Taylor state parks. Among access routes to the national seashore's main visitor center, visitors coming from San Francisco should drive north on U.S. Route 101 to about five miles north of the Golden Gate Bridge, then onto State Route 1 and Bear Valley Road at Olema. West from Petaluma, there are other exits along U.S. Route 101.

Pony Express National Historic Trail

Long Distance Trails Office
National Park Service
P.O. Box 45155
Salt Lake City, UT 84145-0155
801-539-4094

The Pony Express' mail-delivery service is celebrated by this 1,800-mile national historic trail that extends from St. Joseph, Missouri, to Sacramento, California. The service provided ten-day runs from April 1860 to October 1861. This trail is currently in the planning stage by the National Park Service, in cooperation with other governmental agencies and private organizations. Among the many historic highlights along this route are Scotts Bluff National Monument and Chimney Rock National Historic Site in Nebraska and Fort Laramie National Historic Site in Wyoming.

San Francisco Maritime National Historical Park

Lower Fort Mason, Building E
San Francisco, CA 94123-1315
415-556-3002

This 31-acre park along San Francisco's northern waterfront preserves and presents the saga of the people and ships that shaped the development of America's Pacific Coast. Included in this look into maritime history are a fleet of historic boats and ships, including the 19th-century, steel-hulled, square-rigged *Balclutha* built to withstand the rigors of Cape Horn docked at Hyde Street Pier adjacent to Fisherman's Wharf; informative exhibits of artifacts and photographs in the Maritime Museum; grassy Aquatic Park; and the J. Porter Shaw Library of more than 22,000 books, historical documents, and photographs. Ranger-led tours and interpretive films are also available. The annual Festival of the Sea, held during the last week of August, features living history demonstrations, musical programs, and other events.

The park is located at the north end of Hyde Street. Because parking is limited, it is recommended that visitors reach the park by public transit. The Hyde Street cable car line ends at the park and several municipal bus lines serve the area; for information, call 415-673-MUNI.

Santa Monica Mountains National Recreation Area

401 West Hillcrest Drive
Thousand Oaks, CA 91360
818-597-9192

The rugged Santa Monica Mountains extend westward along the Pacific Ocean from Los Angeles to Oxnard in Southern California. Within the overall boundary of the national recreation area are 22,000 acres of scattered National Park Service-administered lands and another 48,000 acres of state and county parklands. The deeply canyon-gashed mountains are largely covered with shrubby chaparral that includes such species as toyon, chamise, manzanita, California scrub oak, and the fragrant-flowering ceanothus. Grassy valley bottoms support open woodlands of valley and coast live oaks, while California sycamores and willows grow along streams. The coastline alternates among rocky shore, narrow sandy beaches, and lagoons.

Among the primary park units are these four areas: 1) Rancho Sierra Vista/Satwiwa and Circle X Ranch, both adjacent to Point Mugu State Park, near the west end of the recreation area; 2) Trancas and Zuma canyons, Rocky Oaks, Peter Strauss Ranch, Castro Crest, and Paramount Ranch areas, the latter two adjoining Malibu Creek State Park in the central part of the recreation area;

3) Topanga State Park and a number of smaller park units at the eastern end of the mountains; and 4) the Cheeseboro and Palo Comado Canyons unit north of U.S. Route 101. The 2,308-acre Palo Comado Canyon property narrowly escaped being turned into a development with a PGA golf course and 12,000 luxury homes by its owner, comedian Bob Hope. But thanks to the political courage and initiative of Maria VanderKolk, a former member of the Ventura County Board of Supervisors, and strong support from NPCA and other environmental groups, Hope was forced to abandon his plans. Negotiations in 1992 led to the sale of the property to the National Park Service.

Visitor activities include hiking, horseback riding, mountain biking, surfing, picnicking, and birdwatching. More than 580 miles of trails wind through the federal, state, and county parks. The Backbone Trail, still being completed, is ultimately expected to extend for 70 miles. The main information center, located at the national recreation area headquarters, provides interpretive exhibits, programs, and publications. Access to the center, which is open daily except on Thanksgiving, Christmas Day, and New Year's Day, is at the Reyes Adobe Road exit from U.S. Route 101 in Agoura Hills. Other interpretive centers are located at the Satwiwa Native American Indian Culture Center and in the Malibu Creek and Topanga state parks. The 55-mile Mulholland Highway runs the length of the national recreation area, and a number of other roads wind through the mountains and canyons between U.S. Route 101 and State Route 1.

Whiskeytown-Shasta-Trinity National Recreation Area

P.O. Box 188
Whiskeytown, CA 96095-0188
916-241-6584

The 42,503-acre Whiskeytown Unit of this national recreation area in northern California was created as water was diverted from the Trinity River Basin to the Sacramento River. With its mountainous backcountry, Whiskeytown Lake, and numerous streams and waterfalls, this area is popular for many water sports and outdoor recreational activities. At the northwest corner is the Tower House

Historic District, in which are the mid-19th-century Camden House (which is open for tours), El Dorado Mine, and stamp mill. The visitor center provides exhibits and publications. Boating, canoeing, water-skiing, swimming, hiking, horseback riding, and mountain biking are among the visitor activities. Ranger-guided walks, gold-panning demonstrations, and evening campfire programs are also offered. Lakeside campgrounds are available; make reservations through National Park Reservation Service at 800-365-CAMP. The Whiskeytown Unit stretches along State Route 299, just west of Shasta. (The Shasta and Trinity units are administered by the U.S. Forest Service.)

GUAM

War in the Pacific National Historical Park

**P.O. Box FA
Agana, GU 96910-9070
671-472-7240**

This 1,960-acre, seven-unit park was established to commemorate the bravery and sacrifice of those participating in the campaigns of the Pacific theater of World War II and to interpret the outstanding historic values and military structures on the Island of Guam, which is part of the North Mariana Islands in the Western Pacific Ocean. The park also protects outstanding natural and scenic areas, including a beautiful beach. Visitor activities include hiking, wind surfing, snorkeling, and scuba diving. The T. Stell Newman Visitor Center, located on Marine Drive in Asan, provides interpretive exhibits and audiovisual programs.

HAWAII

Kalaupapa National Historical Park

**P.O. Box 2222
Kalaupapa, HI 96742-2222
808-567-6802**

This 10,788-acre park contains the site of the Moloka'i Island Hansen's disease (leprosy) settlement, where more than 7,000 persons with the disease were treated and quarantined for life. Many Native Hawaiians were affected by this chronic infectious disease, caused by a bacterium that attacks the skin and other organs of the body. The park, located on the isolated Kalaupapa Peninsula, honors the memory of Father Damien Joseph DeVeuster, a Belgian Roman Catholic priest who devoted the last 12 years of his life (until his death from the disease) to bettering the living conditions of those in the settlement.

In addition, the park protects magnificently rugged coastal, valley, and mountain scenery and habitats that support a number of rare and endangered species. Adjacent to the low-lying peninsula (its name means "flat leaf") are the highest coastal cliffs in the world. Visitors may view the peninsula from Kalaupapa Overlook at the edge of a 1,600-foot cliff. Access to this breathtaking viewpoint is on State Routes 460 and the Kalae Highway (State Route 470) to the Pali Trailhead, where interpretive panels provide information about the history of the colony. Access into the park is by airplane, mule, or on foot. Regulations require that visitors obtain a permit from the Hawaii State Department of Health and join a guided tour. For information on permits and tours, contact Damien Tours, Box 1, Kalaupapa, HI 96742, 808-567-6171, or Ike's Scenic Tours, c/o Kalaupapa Settlement, Kalaupapa, HI 96742.

Kaloko-Honokohau National Historical Park

**73-4786 Kanalani Street, N-14
Kailua Kona, HI 96740-2608
808-329-6881**

This 1,160-acre park on the Kona Coast of the Big Island of Hawaii protects an area of important Hawaiian settlements that were thriving before the arrival of European explorers. The park includes beautiful white sandy beaches, an extensive area of 1,000-year-old barren and jagged black lava flows, and numerous sites of archaeological and historical significance, including two large brackish fishponds. These ponds were but two of more than 100 such centers of Hawaiian Islands aquaculture, providing a carefully regulated, perennial source of food for the people. Kaloko Fishpond, near the northern end of the park,

▲ 'Ai'opio area, Kaloko-Honokohau National Historical Park, Hawaii

was converted from a coastal bay to a pond with the building of a 750-foot-long, 18-foot-high wall of lava boulders. Two sluiceways in the wall were opened to allow fish to be carried into the pond on the incoming tide. The sluiceway was then closed to keep most of the fish from returning to the sea on the outgoing tide. Aimakapa Pond, at the southern end of the park, is contained by a natural barrier beach. Parrotfish, mullet, surgeonfish, goatfish, goby, milkfish, and amberjacks were among the species whose populations were carefully managed to keep the process in balance and prevent overharvesting.

The ponds provide valuable habitat for wildlife, including two endangered birds, the Hawaiian black-necked stilt and Hawaiian coot. Among the flora of the park are coconut palm, heliotrope, orange-flowering kou, noni, and yellow-flowering milo—all of which have long been valued by Native Hawaiians for their wood and medicinal properties. The National Park Service cautions visitors planning to hike in the park to have plenty of drinking water, use sunscreen, and wear a hat, as the sun is normally intense and hot. For hiking across the lava flows, sturdy walking shoes are recommended. Visitors are advised not to swim in the ponds, because of both the ponds' cultural significance and the presence of stinging fire-worms.

While there is presently only a small contact station near Kaloko Fishpond, a visitor center is planned. A picnic area is also located near the fishpond. On Mondays through Fridays, information is available at park headquarters, reached four miles south of Ke-ahole Airport or just north of Honokohau Boat Harbor Road, on State Route 19, then turning onto Hinalani Road and Kanalani Road, into Kaloko Industrial Park. Access to the Kaloko Fishpond area from Route 19 near park headquarters is nearly a mile on a very rough, unpaved road.

93

Pu'uhonua o Hōnaunau National Historical Park

P.O. Box 129
Honaunau, HI 96726-0129
808-328-2326

This 181-acre park on the west coast of the Big Island of Hawaii protects the "Place of Refuge at Honaunau Bay," the largest and most important of many sacred sanctuaries in the Hawaiian Islands. Refuges such as this were for defeated warriors; noncombatants in time of battle, such as the elderly, sick, or injured; and persons who violated ancient laws or taboos (kapu). Since the rule against taking of life was strictly adhered to in a sacred pu'uhonua, lawbreakers who were successful in fleeing to such a safe haven would avoid being put to death to appease the gods. The refuge's priest would then absolve them of their transgressions. This place of refuge, surrounded on two sides by a ten-foot-high stone wall, is a beautiful, coconut palm-shaded site facing the Pacific Ocean. Within the six-acre enclosure is a painstakingly authentic, thatch-roofed reproduction of a temple mausoleum (heiau), similar to the one erected here around 1650. The bones of ruling chiefs were kept in this sacred place known as the House of Keawe, named for the revered ruling chief of the mid-1600s. Standing guard next to the temple are great carved effigies (ki'i), their grotesque expressions designed to scare away unwanted intruders.

The park also contains prehistoric house sites, coconut palm-shaded royal fishponds, and coastal shore with beautiful sandy beaches, black ledges of lava rock, and tidepools filled with intertidal life. Among the birds of the park are common myna, zebra dove, yellow-billed cardinal (with bright red head), Japanese white-eye, and saffron finch.

The visitor center provides interpretive exhibits, programs, and publications, and a self-guided walk leads visitors to key points of interest. A picnic area near the shore is also available. The park occasionally hosts native Hawaiian arts and crafts demonstrations, and on the Friday through Sunday closest to July 1, a Hawaiian festival is held, featuring the colorful Royal Court procession, a ceremony of gift-giving, and court dancers. This annual event is followed by an extensive arts and crafts demonstration and workshop. Access to the park is south of Kailua-Kona, traveling 18.5 miles on State Route 11 and then 3.6 miles on State Route 160.

Puukohola Heiau National Historic Site

P.O. Box 44340
Kawaihae, HI 96743-4340
808-882-7218

High on a hill above the Pacific Ocean, near the village of Kawaihae on the northwest coast of the Big Island of Hawaii, rise the remains of Puukohola Heiau (Temple on the Hill of the Whale)—the last major religious structure of the ancient Hawaiian culture to be built. It was constructed by thousands of laborers under the direction of King Kamehameha the Great during his rise to power in 1790-91 and was dedicated to the king's family god of war, Kuka'ilimoku. Upon the 100-by-224-foot platform of rounded boulders and stones were erected a great altar, a drum house, an oracle tower, a number of thatch-roofed temple structures, and an array of tall, wildly grimacing, carved effigies designed to scare off unwanted intruders. When the temple was completed, Kamehameha invited a long-time rival for control over the Big Island and 11 of his friends to the consecration ceremony. But rather than treating them as guests, he had them killed and offered their bodies as a human sacrifice on the temple altar.

The 86-acre national historic site has a small visitor center with interpretive displays, programs, and publications. A trail leads from the visitor center to a view of the temple, and a road along the shore leads to another view from Samuel M. Spencer Beach Park. Visitors are not permitted to enter the historic platform area. At the site, Hawaiian cultural demonstrations are generally presented one day per week from January through September. Other cultural events are held occasionally and on the Friday through Sunday closest to August 17 the annual Hawaiian Cultural Festival is held. This spectacular event features the colorful Royal Court procession winding down the hill from the temple platform, a gift-presenting ceremony, and court dancers, followed by an extensive arts and crafts demonstration and workshop. (A similar event is held on the Friday through Sunday closest to July 1, at Pu'uhonua o

Hōnaunau National Historical Park.) Along with cultural activities, one of the purposes of the site is to reintroduce native species of flora and expand interpretive programs on traditional native Hawaiian uses of them.

Picnicking and camping are not permitted in the national historic site, but facilities are available in the adjacent Spencer Beach Park. Access to the site is .4 mile north of the intersection of State Routes 19 and 270, on Route 270.

USS *Arizona* Memorial

1 Arizona Memorial Place
Honolulu, HI 96818-3145
808-422-2771

The USS *Arizona* Memorial is the final resting place of this U.S. Navy battleship's 1,177 officers and crew who lost their lives on December 7, 1941, when 343 Japanese bombers, fighters, and torpedo aircraft attacked the U.S. naval base in Pearl Harbor on the island of O'ahu. In the lightning-quick aerial onslaught, 2,403 American sailors, marines, soldiers, and civilians were killed, along with 1,178

Hawaiians. The USS *Arizona* sank after being severely damaged by a bomb; the USS *Oklahoma* and USS *Utah* capsized after being hit by torpedos; three other battleships were sunk and one was purposely run aground to keep them from sinking; and a number of other ships of the Pacific Fleet were heavily damaged. President Franklin D. Roosevelt declared it "a day that shall live in infamy"; and on December 8, Congress declared war on Japan, which caused Germany and Italy to declare war on the United States three days later.

Spanning the mid-portion of the sunken battleship, the 184-foot-long floating memorial structure consists of three main sections: the entry and assembly rooms, a central area designed for general observation and ceremonies, and the shrine room where the names of those who lost their lives on board are engraved on a wall of marble. The memorial, which is open daily, except Thanksgiving, Christmas Day, and New Year's Day, is reached by U.S. Navy boat service from Halawa Landing. From Honolulu and Waikiki, drive west on highway H-1, and take the Arizona Memorial/Stadium exit. Bus service (#20) is also available from Honolulu and Waikiki.

FRIENDS OF THE PARKS ORGANIZATIONS

**Allied Artists of the
Santa Monica Mountains**
117741 Nordhoff
Northbridge, CA 91325
818-886-5170

Citizens for a Mojave National Park
(Mojave National Preserve)
P.O. Box 106
Barstow, CA 92312
619-256-9561

Death Valley 49ers, Inc.
1442 Carson Avenue
Clovis, CA 93611
209-297-5691

Desert Protective Council
P.O. Box 3635
San Diego, CA 92163
619-298-6526

Desert Tortoise Council
(Mojave National Preserve)
P.O. Box 1738
Palm Desert, CA 92261
619-341-8449

Eugene O'Neill Foundation
P.O. Box 402
Danville, CA 94526
925-820-1818

Fort Mason Foundation
Golden Gate National Recreation Area
Fort Mason Center
San Francisco, CA 94123
415-441-5706

**Fort Point and Presidio Historical
Association**
P.O. Box 29163
San Francisco, CA 94129
415-921-8193

Friends of Channel Islands
1901 Spinnaker Drive
Ventura, CA 93001
805-658-5730

Friends of Father Damien
(Kalaupapa National Historical Park)
P.O. Box 6016
Honolulu, HI 96818
808-935-3756

Friends of Fort Point
P.O. Box 29333
San Francisco, CA 94129
415-556-1693

Friends of Pinnacles
122 Parnel Avenue
Santa Cruz, CA 95062
408-427-0740

Friends of Satwiwa
(Santa Monica Mountains
National Recreation Area)
2971 Foothill Drive
Thousand Oaks, CA 91361
805-495-2759

**Golden Gate National Parks
Association**
Building 201, Third Floor
Fort Mason
San Francisco, CA 94123
415-561-3000

Headlands Institute
Golden Gate National Recreation Area
Building 1033
Sausalito, CA 94965
415-332-5771

John Muir Memorial Association
P.O. Box 2433
Martinez, CA 94553
510-228-8860

**Joshua Tree National Park
Association**
74485 National Park Drive
Twentynine Palms, CA 92277
760-367-7488

Kahua Na'au A'o Ma Pu'uhonua o Hōnaunau, Inc.
P.O. Box 788
Honaunau, HI 96726-0788
808-329-6050

Lassen Volcanic National Park Foundation
P.O. Box 8
Mineral, CA 95928
916-898-9309

Las Virgenes Institute
(Santa Monica Mountains
National Receration Area)
4101 Defender Drive
Agoura Hills, CA 91301
818-879-6112

Marine Mammal Center, The
Marin Headlands
Golden Gate National Rrecreation Area
Sausalito, CA 94965
415-289-7325

Mountains Conservancy Foundation
(Santa Monica Mountains National
Rrecreation Area)
3800 Solstice Canyon
Malibu, CA 90265
310-456-7154

Na Aikane o Puukohola Heiau
P.O. Box 2470
Kamuela, HI 96743
808-889-0171

National Maritime Museum Association
(San Francisco Maritime National
Historical Park)
The Presidio, Building 275
San Francisco, CA 91429
415-929-0202

Oregon-California Trails Association
P.O. Box 1019
Independence, MO 64051
816-252-2276

Pacific Crest Trail Conference
P.O. Box 2514
Lynnwood, WA 98036-2514

Santa Monica Mountains Conservancy
5750 Ramirez Canyon Road
Malibu, CA 90265
310-589-3200

Santa Monica Mountains Fund
401 W. Hillcrest Drive
Thousand Oaks, CA 91301
805-370-2329

Santa Monica Mountains Trail Council
24735 Mulholland Highway
Calabasas, CA 91302
818-222-4531

Save-the-Redwoods League
114 Sansome Street, Suite 605
San Francisco, CA 94104-3814
415-362-2352

Sequoia & Kings Canyon National Parks Foundation
Ash Mountain
Three Rivers, CA 93271
209-565-3727

Yosemite Association
P.O. Box 230
El Portal, CA 95318
209-379-2646

Yosemite Fund, The
155 Montgomery Street, Suite 1104
San Francisco, CA 94104
415-434-1782

Yosemite Institute
P.O. Box 487
Yosemite, CA 95389
209-372-9300

Yosemite Restoration Trust
1212 Broadway, Suite 814
Oakland, CA 94612
510-763-1403

Cooperating Associations

Arizona Memorial Museum Association
USS _Arizona_ Memorial
1 _Arizona_ Memorial Place
Honolulu, HI 98818
808-422-2771

Cabrillo Historical Association
P.O. Box 6870
San Diego, CA 92106
619-557-5450

Death Valley Natural History Association
P.O. Box 188
Death Valley, CA 92328
760-786-3285

Hawaii Natural History Association
P.O. Box 74
Hawaii Volcanoes National Park, HI 96718
808-985-6000

Joshua Tree Natural History Association
74485 National Park Drive
Twentynine Palms, CA 92277
760-367-7488

Lava Beds Natural History Association
P.O. Box 865
Tulelake, CA 96134
530- 667-2282

Loomis Museum Association
Lassen Volcanic National Park
P.O. Box 100
Mineral, CA 96063
530-595-3262

National Trust for Historic Preservation
1785 Massachusetts Avenue, NW
Washington, DC 20036
202-673-4000

Point Reyes National Seashore Association
Point Reyes, CA 94956
415-663-1155

Redwood Natural History Association
1111 Second Street
Crescent City, CA 95531
707-434-9150

Sequoia Natural History Association
HCR 89, Box 10
Three Rivers, CA 93271
559-565-3758

Southwest Parks and Monuments Association
211 N. Court Avenue
Tucson, AZ 85701
520-622-1999

Student Conservation Association
1800 N. Kent Street
Arlington, VA 22209
703-524-2441

LOCAL COLOR

The Wildlife

"Texas" means friend.

Texas was a country before it was a state.

25 languages.

65 nationalities.

Texans believe life is too important to be dull.

The Wildflowers

The state flower is the Bluebonnet.

Over 5,000 species of wildflowers.

There's even a Wildflower Center (Thanks to Lady Bird Johnson).

Texas does not have blue grass. It just seems that way.

It's like a whole other country.®

Even the vacations are bigger in Texas. From the yarn-spinning charm of our native citizenry to hills carpeted with our native flowers, you'll find it all in Texas. It's more than you think. It's like a whole other country. For your free Texas travel guide, you can visit our web site at 🖥 **www.TravelTex.com** or call us at ☎ **1-800-8888-TEX (Ext. 1290).** So give us a call, y'all.